YO-BSX-711

Acknowledgements

I would like to thank *Nancy Eckman* for her countless hours of reading, suggesting, editing and even typing, all of which helped to make this book the best book I could write.

I also want to thank my staff assistant *Tami Belmont* for her reading, comments and help in editing. *Janet Geston*, my editor, did an extraordinary job in keeping my book grammatically accurate.

I especially appreciate the time my wife *Jodi* and son *Grant* allowed me to write this book.

Also by Dan Geffre

Any Questions? Answers for Basic Investing

Copyright 1998 - Dan Geffre
All rights reserved.

Printed in the United States of America

ISBN - 0-9651517-1-9

First Printing - 1998

THE INVE$TOR FOR LIFE

Dan Geffre

Table of Contents

Chapter 1: Understanding the Economy

The performance of investments will be influenced by what is happening in the economy. Bond and stock returns vary depending on corporate profits, interest rates, investor psychology and many other factors. Conflicting reports are frequently issued, giving analysts different readings and interpretations of the direction our economy is headed. There are almost as many economic theories as there are economists. No one has been consistently accurate predicting the short-term direction of our economy. Two things are certain, however: the economy always cycles and no cycle is the same. The *'this time it's different'* argument is only accurate in that no two cycles are the same. You can be sure that the economy will always cycle.

The general direction of our economy can be helpful for us to formulate an investment strategy that will allow us to take advantage of present investment opportunities. Let's examine a few important macro-economic relationships that exist.

One of the questions many people ask is how the stock markets and interest rates are related. The answer is, generally... inversely. In other words,

When interest rates rise, stock prices decline ... temporarily.

When interest rates fall, stock prices rise ...

Take a look at a simplified example.
Let's assume that I own a store that sells a product that you like and use regularly. You come into my store weekly and buy a lot of my

products. Let's also assume that my store is located in Fargo, ND, where the winters can be quite cold and windy.

As the business owner, I have been raising the prices of my products around 2½% per year. Recently, however, I have decided that the winters have become a little more challenging than I care to experience, so I decide to build a house in Arizona.

To build this home, I'm going to need a little extra income. I decide this year I am going to raise the prices of my products 4% over last year's prices. This extra profit should be enough to pay for my new home. Of course it isn't. You know what they say: when you build a house, it always costs more than you planned. That is also the case for my Arizona home. Because it is costing me more to build than I thought, I decide to raise my prices 6% the following year so I have more profits.

In the meantime, however, watching over this entire process is the Federal Reserve. The Federal Reserve System is comprised of twelve regional banks. Its main function is to regulate the nation's banking system and to control the nation's money supply (control interest rates). The Fed accomplishes its objectives through monetary supply. Monetary policy attempts to control the supply of money and credit in the economy. This will affect interest rates, causing an increase or decrease in economic activity. *The Fed's top priority is to control inflation.*

Because the Fed doesn't want Americans' standard of living to decrease, it keeps a vigilant eye on the costs of living. The Fed notices my prices rising at a rate of 6%, and they don't like it. Why? Because they did a survey and found that workers' increase in salary is averaging about 2½% to 3% per year. If the costs of the products that you buy are rising at 6% and your paycheck is rising at 2½%, your standard of living is going down. The Fed does not want this to continue.

What does the Fed do? Basically, they start raising interest rates (they take money out of the economy). Once interest rates begin rising, what do your spending habits do? Right, they slow down. When interest rates go up, people will generally put off spending on many items because they can no longer afford many things. It now costs more to borrow money. We are more likely to put off major purchases such as buying a car or a home when interest rates are high.

If your spending slows down, that means you will be coming into my store less and, consequently, my profits will begin to decline. If my profits decline because you are coming into my store less, my company's stock price will decline. A company's stock price is a reflection of the value and profitability of the company. When interest rates rise, people spend less, companies' profits decline and their stock price reflects this lower profitability. **When interest rates rise, stock prices decline** ... temporarily.

Now the Fed doesn't want to punish me too harshly. Why? The economy cannot afford to have all companies go bankrupt because it is these companies, like mine, who employ you. If the Fed keeps interest rates too high, too long, my business will suffer to the degree that I will have to start laying off people. They don't want my company to go out of business; they just want me to stop raising prices so much.

Now as a business owner, I get the hint (from the Fed). I stop raising my prices so much and the Fed rewards this by lowering interest rates (adding money back into the economy) to stimulate purchasing by consumers. Remember, the government cannot afford for me to go out of business. I employ you and they need the taxes.

As interest rates fall, you decide to start spending more and begin shopping at my store again. Consequently, my profits begin to rise. Because stock prices reflect increased value and profitability, my stock price rises. **When interest rates fall, stock prices rise.**

That's basically how the economy works. Interest rates rise and fall based on current and future expected inflation. Stock prices change based on current and future expected earnings. Take a look at the shaded areas in the following graph through March 1998:

Short-Term Relationship of Interest Rates and the Stock Market
1980 - 1998

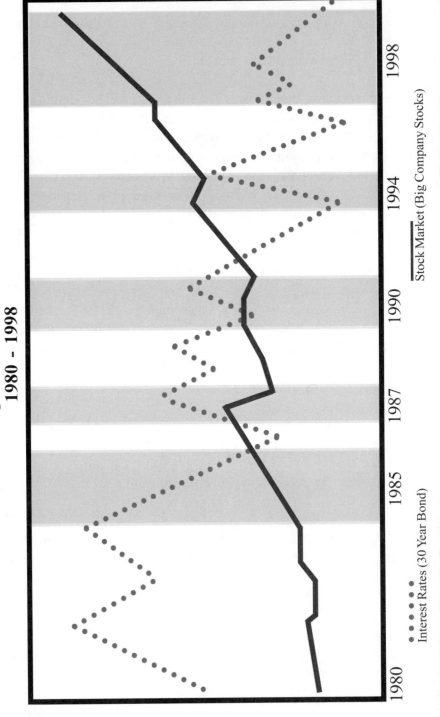

1980   1985   1987   1990   1994   1998

•••• Interest Rates (30 Year Bond)

—— Stock Market (Big Company Stocks)

As you can see, there is a clear relationship between stock prices and interest rates over short periods of time. Over longer periods of time, however, interest rates fluctuate up and down while stock prices continue to rise.

Back to my story, the Fed's point of view of how the economy works is not quite that simple. The government periodically issues economic indicators which gives investors and the Federal Reserve an idea of the direction in which the economy is moving. The Fed then analyzes these indicators and takes appropriate actions to try keeping the economy growing while maintaining a rising standard of living.

The Fed looks at a number of indicators such as the Consumer Price Index (CPI), Producer Price Index (PPI), the unemployment report, the payroll employment figure, the index of leading economic indicators, housing starts and many other indicators. Most of these figures are reported on a monthly basis.

There are other indicators that monitor the health and direction of the economy. Most investors don't have enough time or expertise to make heads or tails of all of them. That is the job of the Fed, economists and brokerage house analysts. A general feel for the direction of the economy, however, will help give you a broad direction to pursue as your investment portfolio grows over time.

Chapter 2: Fixed Income Investments

Rather than spend a lot of time distinguishing the differences between fixed income investments, I'd rather spend the time giving you the basics of how bonds work and why they may or may not fit into your investment portfolio. Also, this fixed income business is so boring I was afraid you might stop reading here! So, I will keep it as short as I can.

Fixed income investments pay you interest, or income, on a periodic schedule for the use of your money. Unlike growth investments, whose returns fluctuate, income investments offer the stability of knowing exactly how much interest you will receive until your investment matures. Your fixed income investment will pay a certain rate of interest that will not change until maturity.

There are many types of fixed income investments such as Treasury securities, corporate bonds, junk bonds, convertible bonds, municipal bonds and others. Let's *briefly* summarize their characteristics.

Treasury securities are the means by which the U.S. government borrows money. Their bonds come in three different forms distinguished by their maturities. Treasury *bills* come in three, six, and twelve-month maturities. Treasury *notes* have maturities of more than one year and less than ten years. Treasury *bonds* have maturities ranging from more than ten years all the way to thirty years.

Corporate bonds are IOUs issued by a public corporation. They work much the same as when you go to the bank to buy a CD. When you buy a CD, you are loaning your money to the bank, which then takes that money and uses it to finance its outgoing loans. The same is true of bonds. You give your money to the corporation and it agrees to pay your money back at a certain time in the future, including interest. The company will use the money to finance its operations. It may pay off other loans, buy more products, or use it to expand.

Junk bonds are high-yield bonds with very high interest rates that are issued by corporations . They pay high interest rates because there is a strong possibility that the issuing company may not be able to earn enough money to pay its interest payments. Junk bonds earn a low grade from bond rating services like Standard & Poor's or Moody's. The biggest risk in owning these bonds is default. Be sure you know what you are doing if you decide to buy this type of bond!

Convertible bonds, some would say, are the best of both worlds. A convertible bond pays a fixed rate of interest for a fixed period of time. However, the bond buyer has the right to convert the bond into a certain number of common stock shares of the issuing company. If the company does well and its stock price rises, the bondholder can convert the bond into the stock and participate in the company's growth. If the company doesn't do so great and the stock goes nowhere, you will still have the security of collecting regular interest payments from the convertible bond.

Municipal bonds (popularly called *munis*) are one of the few remaining sources of tax-free income. Cities, states, and other local bodies and political subdivisions issue these bonds. The interest on the munis is unique. It is not subject to federal income taxes and may also be exempt from state and local taxes if you buy munis that are issued from your own state.

There are two basic types of municipal bonds: *general obligation* and *revenue* bonds. Their classification comes from their payment source. There is an important distinction.

General obligation bonds pay their interest from the revenues of the cities or states. The full faith and credit of the state or local government that has taxing power secure the payments of principal and interest on general obligation bonds. General obligation bonds are typically secured by the government's unlimited taxing power. That gives them a higher priority and level of safety than revenue bonds.

Revenue bonds are payable from a specific source of money - usually the charges, tolls or rents from the facility being built. Highways, bridges, airports, hospitals, and water and sewer treatment plants are typical examples. Because the backing power of the bonds doesn't come from taxes but rather from the *revenues* of the project, this type of municipal bond may be considered more risky than general obligation bonds and consequently may offer higher yields.

Let's take a look at how taxes affect your investment's real returns. Let's assume an investor is in a 31% federal tax bracket and compare returns on two different investments - one, a federal and state tax-free municipal bond paying 6% and two, a taxable income investment like a corporate bond or CD paying 7%. Notice the substantial effect taxes have on your after-tax return.

CD/Corporate Bond (7%)		*Tax-Free Municipal Bond (6%)*	
$100,000	Principal	$100,000	Principal
7.00%	Interest Rate	6.00%	Interest Rate
$7,000	Income Earned	$6,000	Income Earned
$7,000	Income Earned	$6,000	Income Earned
31%	Income Tax Rate	0%	Income Tax Rate
$2,170	Income Taxes Paid	$0	Income Taxes Paid
$7,000	Income Earned	$6,000	Income Earned
$2,170	Income Taxes Paid	$0	Income Taxes Paid
$4,830	**After-Tax Income**	**$6,000**	**After-Tax Income**

Some investors simply buy municipal bonds with the intention of avoiding paying taxes to the government. This may not always be the wisest decision. The higher your tax bracket, the bigger the tax advantages become. If you are in a lower tax bracket, your taxable equivalent spread becomes much less advantageous.

Before you buy tax-free bonds, figure out how the yield compares with the after-tax return you could get on alternative investments. It is not how little tax you pay, but how much you will have after taxes over a period of time that will determine which is your best choice.

Private insurers such as the Municipal Bond Insurance Association (MBIA), the American Municipal Bond Assurance Corporation (AMBAC) and others insure some municipal securities' principal and interest against default. The insured municipal bonds' yields are generally slightly lower than non-insured bonds because the costs of the insurance are passed on to the bondholder.

As with any other investment, if you buy only the highest quality municipals, the chances of default are very, very low. If, however, the insurance will help you rest at night, then perhaps insured bonds would be well worth consideration.

How the Interest Rate is Determined on Bonds

Market forces such as the issuer's credit standing, the length of maturity, current interest rate conditions and other variables determine the interest rate offered by a bond issuer (corporation). There are two basic ingredients that determine a bond's interest rate: *maturity* and *quality*.

Maturity is the length of time you are lending your money to the issuer. If you lend your money for ten years, you are taking a different risk than if you lend it for one year. Short-term rates are generally lower than long-term rates. A one-year bond will pay a lower rate of interest than a ten-year bond.

If you are willing to lend your money for a longer period of time, you will usually get a higher rate of interest because of potential economic changes in the future. To compensate for locking up your money for intermediate and long-term maturities, issuers are forced to offer you higher interest rates than for short-term maturities because of risk that interest rates might be higher in the future. In general, the longer the maturity date, the higher your interest rate will be.

There is one exception to this rule: when the Federal Reserve decides to restrict credit, short-term rates surge as borrowers scramble to obtain money. In this case, the yield curve becomes inverted, and temporarily, short-term rates exceed the long-term interest rates. The purpose of the rise in short-term interest rates is to cool off the economy and help lower inflation. If the Fed keeps these short-term rates too high for too long, the result could lead to a recession.

The *quality* of the issuer also determines what it must pay to borrow your money. The issue here is simple. How certain are you that the issuer will pay you back your principal with interest as scheduled? If the issuer has a lower credit rating because of poor business conditions or has a short track record of earnings and sales, it may have to offer a higher interest rate to attract money to compensate for additional risk. A financially secure company with the highest credit rating will pay less than a corporation with a lesser quality rating.

That's why you see a difference in the interest rate that two different issuers offer with the same maturity. For example, a five-year corporate bond would need to offer a higher rate of interest to attract your money than would a five-year government note. There is less perceived risk in loaning your money to the government than to a corporation.

When you are trying to decide on which type of bonds to buy, not only must you be prepared to hold the bond until maturity, but you must also consider the amount of quality risk you are willing to assume. If you won't consider anything but "guaranteed" bonds such as

Treasuries, you must also be willing to accept lower rates of return than your peers who are willing to assume a little quality risk to earn a higher rate of return.

How Bonds Work

It may be surprising to learn that bond prices fluctuate just as stock prices do. Bonds are priced differently than stocks, however. Bonds are priced with a face value of $1,000. So ten bonds would equal $10,000 worth of bonds. But, because bond prices fluctuate with interest rates, their current value may be different than the original $1,000 face value. Depending on current interest rates, bonds may be priced at par, premium or discount. Here are some examples:

Par	=	$1,000
Premium	=	$1,070
Discount	=	$980

Essentially what happens is that as interest rates and economic conditions change, so do the prices of bonds. They fluctuate during the life of the bond. At some time, the price of the bonds may be at a discount or a premium depending on the prevailing interest rates.

When Interest Rates Rise, Bond Prices Fall ... Temporarily
When Interest Rates Fall, Bond Prices Rise ... Temporarily

Why?

Let's say you bought a bond at par ($1,000) and it was paying 7% interest. Then, one year later, interest rates started rising and the same kind of bond offered one year later was paying 8%. How would that temporarily affect the principal value of your 7% bond? It would make it look less attractive because people can now earn a higher rate of interest (8%) than your own bond paying 7%. If you wanted to sell your 7% bond, you would get less than par because the bond is less attractive. If you sold it prior to maturity, depending on prevailing higher interest rates, you would get less than you put in, and you would be forced to sell at a discount.

Conversely, if interest rates fell a year later to 6%, your 7% bond would become more valuable and you could then choose to sell the bond at a premium because of its attractive interest rate.

If you plan to hold your bond until maturity, it really doesn't matter where your bond price trades during its life (as long as the issuer doesn't go bankrupt). The issuer has promised to pay back $1,000 per bond at maturity. Only when you are forced to sell your bond *before* maturity do the premium or discount fluctuations become important.

Let me repeat: If you hold your bond until maturity, the issuer promises to pay back par value ($1,000) for the bond. Let's say you buy 10 premium bonds at a cost of $10,500. If you held them to maturity, the issuer would pay you par for the bonds. So you would get back $10,000 plus interest during the life of the bond. The $500 premium you paid for the bond would be amortized during the bond's life until, at maturity, the bond would be priced at par ($10,000).

You paid $10,500 and got back $10,000. Doesn't sound like too good of a deal does it? But the bonds were priced at a premium because they paid a higher rate of interest than the current new bonds being offered. Ultimately, you earned more interest during the life of this bond than did others that bought the lower-interest-paying new bonds. The extra interest you earned made up for the $500 premium you paid. *The bottom line is that you've earned about the same total return as bondholders buying bonds today at the current interest rates.*

Conversely, if you bought bonds at a discount you might, say, pay $9,500. At maturity, the issuer would give you back par value or $10,000 plus interest earned during the life of the bond. You received an extra $500 because of the discount price you paid. However, the reason the bonds may have been at a discount is that they paid a lower interest rate. Your total return would be about the same as the new bonds.

Risks Associated with Bonds

As with any other investment, there are risks associated with bonds. Outside of the most obvious risk - inflation risk - there are two other basic risks involved with bonds: *default* risk and *interest rate* risk.

The most obvious way you can lose principal is when the issuer *defaults* on the bonds. In other words, the issuer doesn't have the ability to pay back your principal for the bonds. It doesn't happen very often, but it can.

Before you buy any bond, you should check the credit quality of the issuer. You can do this by consulting a number of rating agencies like Moody's and Standard & Poor's. These rating agencies assign a credit rating based on the financial condition of the issuer offering the bonds. Unless you're speculating, most investors should stay with bonds that have a quality rating of AAA or AA.

Investors willing to assume more risk would consider lower-quality issues such as bonds rated BBB (lowest investment grade). These bonds offer yields of 1% to 2% higher than bonds rated AAA (highest rating of safety). Bonds which are rated BB+ or lower are considered junk bonds and they offer even higher yields, but carry with them considerably more default risk.

The other way to lose money in bonds is *interest rate* risk. Let's go back to the mid-1970s when long-term government bonds were being offered at 8%. About five years later, or by the early 1980s, inflation was running rampant at a rate of 12-13% and the government was forced to offer their long-term bonds at a rate much higher than normal. By 1980, you could buy that same bond at par and earn 14%! If you needed to sell that 8% bond, no one would give you par for the bond paying 8% because now they could pay par for a bond that was paying 14%. If you were forced to sell, you would only have been offered about $700 for each bond. That's a loss of $300 from your original investment of $1,000 per bond if you had to sell.

That is what happens to all bonds when interest rates rise. The longer the term of the bond, the more fluctuation it will be subject to. It has nothing to do with quality or its interest paying ability. It's simply that as interest rates rise, there are comparable bonds available with higher returns. Remember, *when interest rates rise, bond prices fall, temporarily*.

This rule holds true with all bonds including corporate, government, and municipal bonds and even bonds in mutual funds and unit investment trusts. You must be even more careful when buying bonds when interest rates are low. The lower the interest rate, the higher the probability that interest rates will be moving higher in the future which will force down the value of your bonds.

At any time, it is impossible to predict interest rates with any great accuracy. If you wish to invest in bonds, the wisest course is to spread your money over a range of maturities, from as short as one or two years to no longer than ten or 15 years. By staggering maturities over time in this fashion, you will soon have money coming available that can be reinvested if interest rates go up. And if interest rates fall instead, you will have the satisfaction of owning a large number of bonds that are earning considerably more than the market is currently offering.

Some companies may choose to pay off all the bonds they've issued before the stated maturity in case interest rates drop sharply. This is called a *call provision*. This call provision allows the issuer to reissue new bonds at a new lower interest rate. This provision is very similar to the option that homeowners have with their own home mortgage. If interest rates decline substantially from your current mortgage rate, you have the right to re-finance your home mortgage at a lower rate. The same is true for bond issuers. If a company has this feature in its bond issue, it will be stated in the bond agreement. This agreement will describe the date, schedule and price at which the bond may be called in from you. You should check to see if the bond you're considering has this feature before you buy it.

Pros & Cons of Fixed Income

Why are there so many differing opinions today regarding the benefits of fixed income investments such as CDs, and corporate, treasury and municipal bonds? A number of factors need to be considered.

Most significantly, there have been changes both in the age at which people retire and in their life expectancy. Anyone choosing an early or normal retirement may look forward to at least another 20 years of life. The risk? The rising cost of living for such a long period of time.

Many advisors recommend investors diversify with bonds because they generally fluctuate less. However, the interest rate environment of the middle and late 1990s has made fixed income investments less attractive. Consequently, there is much contradictory advice.

Clearly, bonds are more attractive when interest rates are high. When buying bonds while interest rates are high, investors can lock in the attractive rate for a long period of time and not have to worry about declining interest rates. If they do decline, the older bond's price will temporarily rise, giving the bondholder the opportunity to sell the bond for a profit.

On the other hand, the least attractive time to buy bonds is when interest rates are low. Not only are you investing your money at a low rate for an extended period of time, but also the risk of a rising interest rate environment is greater. The lower interest rates are the higher the probability that rates will be rising in the future.

This leads me to the pros and cons of fixed income investments. Then, I will offer their strongest advantage.

Pros	**Cons**
Guarantee of Principal at Maturity	Guarantee of Principal at Maturity
Guarantee of Fixed Interest	Guarantee of Fixed Interest

Is this a misprint? No.

A *guarantee of principal at maturity* is a ***pro*** in the sense that you will know that you will get the exact same *currency* at maturity as you put in, say ten years ago. But at the same time, it is a ***con*** in that the principal is worth a lot less ten years later because of the rising costs of living (inflation). $10,000 will not buy nearly as much today as it did ten years ago.

The *guarantee of a fixed interest payment* is a ***pro*** especially when interest rates are high (which isn't very often). Investors will know exactly what interest they will get for the term of the bond or CD and that the interest will not change during its life. The ***con***? The *interest is fixed*! If you don't have costs of living (medical, food, clothing, entertainment etc.) that are fixed, how can you have interest that is fixed and never rises? You can't, unless you have more money than you will ever need or interest rates are exorbitantly high and you lock in those rates forever.

So when are bonds most attractive? When interest rates are high. If investors are astute enough to determine when interest rates are high relative to history and inflation, bonds can be a very good value.

In the end, the purpose of fixed income investments like CDs and bonds (excluding high interest rate times) is that they will provide some reduced fluctuation to a diversified portfolio. A portfolio that includes bonds with stocks will generally fluctuate less than if it contained only stocks. For example, look at the hypothetical difference between a 50% stock 50% fixed income portfolio and a 100% stock portfolio in a down period.

Fixed Income Investments

$$\text{Stocks} \quad = \quad -20\%$$

$$\text{Fixed Income} \quad = \quad -10\%$$

50/50 Stock/Fixed Income Portfolio	100% Stock Portfolio
-15%	-20%

As you can see, the diversified portfolio with fixed income assets declined less than the all-stock portfolio. This reduced fluctuation is the biggest advantage of a diversified portfolio.

What is the cost to this reduced fluctuation? By reducing the downside fluctuation, you inevitably reduce some of the upside returns of an all-stock portfolio. If we look at the long-term averages of stocks and fixed income assets and factor in the reduced upside potential, what could we expect?

$$\text{Stocks} \quad = \quad +10\%$$
$$\text{CDs/Bonds} \quad = \quad +5\%$$

50/50 Stock/Fixed Income Portfolio	100% Stock Portfolio
+ 7 % p/yr	+10% p/yr

As you can see, the cost to that reduced fluctuation is about +3% per year of permanent positive annual returns. This will be substantial over longer periods of time. Moreover, since stocks decline significantly about once every 3 ½ years on average, fixed income assets will generally be most advantageous about once every four years.

Investors must decide for themselves how much short-term, temporary declines will affect them. If the extra 5% or 10% temporary decline would make you too nervous to sleep at night, then owning fixed income assets would make sense. They will reduce *some* downward fluctuation.

Chapter 3: Stocks

The stock market has been a real hero for a large number of investors and a real sore spot for others. You will hear countless stories of people who make a killing in the market and others who lost their shirts. While some of these tales may be true, the simple fact is that if you are a long-term investor, the probability of your money outperforming inflation and taxes with stocks is much greater than with any other type of investment. That's the goal of most investors – to create a higher standard of living for the future. Stocks are the only investment that have consistently outpaced taxes and inflation.

Understanding Stocks

A share of stock represents ownership in a corporation. A corporation is owned by its stockholders – often thousands of people and institutions, each owning a fraction of the corporation.

When you buy a stock in a corporation, you become a part owner or stockholder. You immediately own a part, no matter how small, of every building, piece of office furniture, machinery, or whatever that company owns.

As a shareholder, you stand to profit when the company profits. You are also legally entitled to a say in major policy decisions, such as whether to issue additional stock, sell the company to outside buyers, or change the board of directors. The general rule is that each share has the same voting power, so the more shares you own, the greater your power.

You can vote in person by attending a corporation's annual meeting. Or you can vote by using an absentee ballot, called a *proxy*, which is mailed before each meeting.

A stock does not have a fixed, objective worth. At any moment, it's only as valuable as people think it is. When you buy a stock, you're making a bet that a lot of other people are going to want to buy that stock too – and, as a result, the price will go up.

The stock market is, however, more than a lot of investors watching what other investors do. Investors and analysts also watch the companies and their future prospects very carefully. Since the value of shares is directly related to how well the company is doing, investors naturally look for the companies with the best prospects for strong, sustained earnings.

How do you judge a company's prospects? By current or anticipated earnings, the desirability of its product or service, the competition, availability of new markets, management strengths and many other considerations. These are the factors that stock analysts watch in trying to predict whether a stock's value will rise or fall.

How do you make money in stocks? As a rule, the better a company does and the higher its profits, the more money its stockholders make. Investors buy stocks to make money in one or both of the following ways:

    1) Through dividend payments while you own the stock,
    2) By selling the stock for more than you paid.

Most companies parcel out portions of their annual profits to stockholders in the form of quarterly *dividend payments*. Dividend payments vary from stock to stock. Companies with consistent histories of paying high dividends are known as *income stocks*. Investors buy income stocks for their current dividends rather than for the company's future growth prospects.

Some companies, however, reinvest most of their profits back into their business in order to expand and strengthen. As a result, companies that pay little or no dividend are called *growth stocks* because investors expect the company to grow – and the stock price to grow with it.

When stocks are traded in the market, the company doesn't make a cent on the deal. A company only makes money when the new stock is issued, or put up for sale. The first time a company's stock is issued, the company is said to be *going public*. In other words, the owners of the company are selling part ownership to the general public. The formal name for this process is an *initial public offering* (IPO).

Why do companies issue stock? Typically, a company offers stock when it needs to raise money, usually for expansion. In exchange for the cash, the company management gives up some of the decision-making control to the shareholders. When a company goes public, it also benefits from the fact that its stock is trading in the open market. This trading tends to give the company legitimacy: its performance, its financial vitality, becomes visible to all.

Bull or Bear?

The stock market goes through cycles, trending upward for periods of time, then reversing itself temporarily, and vice versa. A rising period is known as a ***bull market*** – bulls being the market optimists who cause prices to rise. A ***bear market*** is a falling or flat stock market, where the pessimists are driving prices lower.

The stock market is a constant struggle between the bulls and the bears, both groups tugging in opposite directions. Inevitably, however, the bulls win the struggle as the stock market always eventually rises over longer periods of time. Sometimes market trends last a long time, even years. Overall, though, bull markets usually continue for longer periods of time than bear markets.

Common Stock

Common stock owners typically are entitled to vote on the selection of directors and other important matters as well as to receive dividends on their holdings. In the event that a corporation is liquidated, the claims of secured and unsecured creditors and owners of bonds and preferred stock take precedence over the claims of those who own common stock. For the most part, common stock has more potential for appreciation.

Preferred Stock

Preferred stock pays dividends at a specified rate and has preference over common stock in the payment of dividends and the liquidation of assets. The dividend is usually higher than the common stock dividend.

The term "preferred" does not mean "better". It relates only to dividend precedence. Preferred stock does not ordinarily carry voting rights. If the preferred stock is also convertible to common stock, it will have a conversion ratio into the common and take some of the characteristics of the company's common stock.

Types of Stocks by Performance

If you wanted to maximize your growth potential, you might want to take a look at *growth stocks*. Growth stocks are stocks that show a better-than-average appreciation over a period of time. Their sales, earnings and market share are expanding faster than the general economy and the industry average. The key to success is picking these stocks in advance of their strongest period of growth. Because of their uncertainty, growth stocks are called speculative and their price may fluctuate a great deal. These stocks are characterized by low dividend yields and high price/earnings (PE) ratios.

To be successful at selecting growth stocks, you must be aware of current events. Consumer psychology plays a big part in the evaluation of growth stocks. You must also keep track of which industries are presently most dominant. These industries are where the most growth will come from and, thus, where many of the stock market's biggest winners will emerge.

You will need to look for companies with consistent annual increasing growth in earnings and sales, even in the face of poor economic conditions. These companies normally have a new product or service that people need or want.

Some people prefer to stick only with big-name companies with proven sales and track records. *Blue chip stocks* make a good choice for those who want to invest their money in a well-known company that has demonstrated its ability to pay dividends in good and bad times.

The term *blue chip* was introduced in the early 1900s to describe the stocks of the largest, most consistently profitable corporations. They are the common stocks of nationally known companies that have a long record of profit growth and dividend payments and a reputation for high-quality management and services.

If you are looking for the next stock to double in a very short period of time, a *special situation stock* might give you the best chance. A special situation stock is stock in a company whose potential is not reflected in its day-to-day operations. A new management team, a technological breakthrough or similar occurrence can cause speculation for new growth in the future.

Some stocks do relatively well regardless of the economic times. *Defensive stocks* are not subject to the variations of the business cycle. They have resistance to a recession. Examples are food chains, utilities and tobacco companies. People will use gas and electricity and smoke during bad economic periods as well as during good times.

If you are looking for a stock that pays a higher rate of current dividend yield, you might consider an *income stock*. Its dividends are high relative to the market price. This type of stock is generally attractive to those who buy stocks for current income.

If you are dependent on income for your groceries and if the price of groceries continues to rise, you must increase your income to keep pace with the rise in food prices. Many income stocks have raised their dividends (income) year after year for many years. This type of stock investment makes a lot of sense for people who need a rising income stream to keep pace with inflation. Most public utilities and real estate investment trusts (REITs) are considered income stocks.

It is important that you don't reach too far for high yields in income stocks, however. Normally, the reason a stock's yield is abnormally high is that the company is paying out an inordinately large percentage of its earnings. Another reason a stock may have an unusually high yield is that the market has given the company a poor evaluation for future prospects. You may be risking your capital because the stock's price may fall considerably. In other words, if it looks too good to be true, it probably is!

In selecting stocks for dependable income, you'll want to choose quality issues with long, established dividend records rather than younger, less tested companies who haven't been in business long enough to establish an extended dividend paying record.

Some stocks coming out of a recession do better than others. *Cyclical stocks* are stocks of companies whose earnings fluctuate with the general business cycle. If you were looking to maximize your stock returns and wanted to take advantage of the rise in the economy's profitability, these cyclical stocks might be a good choice.

When business conditions improve, the company's profitability is restored and the common stock price rises. When economic conditions deteriorate, the company's business falls off and its profits are diminished. This causes the cyclical stock's price to decline. Steel, cement, machine tools and automobiles are some of the groups of stocks you might look for to find investments that fit into your portfolio.

Finally, can you believe that stocks can change with the weather? Some stocks have seasonal changes; they are called *seasonal stocks*. These are stocks of companies whose earnings have a tendency to fluctuate with the year's seasons. Retail companies represent a good example. Their sales and profits will generally increase at certain times of the year, such as Christmas and the opening of school.

Stock Characteristics

If you take the number of shares of stock outstanding of a company and multiply that number by the stock's current price, you will find the total market value of that company. If a company has 500 million shares outstanding and each share is worth $20, then the market value of that company is $10 billion. This is one way to compare the size of two companies.

To determine how well a company may be doing, look at its *sales*. If a company's sales are increasing, there is a good possibility that the company is earning money. Analysts look at the sales that are reported on a quarterly basis and compare them to last year's sales figures. If the sales increases meet or exceed expectations, the stock's price normally rises. This figure is just one of many used to determine the value of a company.

Another is to look at a company's *earnings*. Publicly traded companies calculate and report their earnings quarterly (every three months). Analysts and stock buyers watch for the earnings figure to see how well it compares with last year's quarterly earnings. If the earnings reported are better than last year's or better than expected, the company's stock price normally rises. If the company reports poor earnings for the quarter, its stock price normally drops.

Stock analysts take the earnings reported and divide that number by the number of shares outstanding to get a number called the *earnings per share*. This figure represents how much money the company is making per share of stock outstanding.

Another figure stock buyers and analysts look at is the stock's price/ earnings ratio (P/E ratio). The P/E ratio is the price of a share of stock divided by earnings per share for a 12-month period. In other words, it's the price of a stock relative to its earnings. If a stock has a price of $50 and is earning $2.50 a share, it is said to be selling at a P/E ratio of 20 to 1. In other words, its selling price is 20 times last year's earnings and its P/E is 20.

A general rule to follow is that the Dow Jones Industrial Average and the S & P 500's P/E ratio historically ranges around 15 to 18. It can fluctuate greatly, and it does in extreme times. Smaller growth companies have higher future growth and earnings expectations; it follows that this type of company has a higher P/E ratio. The more mature, slower-growing companies tend to have a lower P/E ratio.

One cautionary note: A low P/E ratio doesn't necessarily mean that a company is undervalued and a high P/E ratio doesn't necessarily mean that the company is overpriced. There are reasons why stocks have high prices and low prices; these don't include that it's simply a great buy or a time to sell. Stocks usually sell for what they're worth at that time.

Out of a company's earnings come dividends. Dividends are to stocks what interest is to bonds/CDs. A dividend is the term used to describe a payment to shareholders. Most people are familiar with dividends paid by utility companies. But a large number of other companies also pay a dividend.

Dividends are paid out of a company's earnings. For example, let's say a company paid a total annual $2 dividend per share. If you owned 100 shares of that company, you would get a dividend payment of

$200 for the year. Dividends are paid on a quarterly basis. In the previous case, every three months you would receive a dividend check for $50 ($50 x 4 = $200).

If you had invested $5,000 in a stock and it pays you a dividend of $200, you would be receiving a 4% dividend return. Of course, the value of the stock can move up or down; that changes your total return.

Companies declare their dividends ahead of time. The interval between the announcement of the dividend and the actual payment date is called the ex-dividend date. An investor who buys shares during that interval is not entitled to the dividend. You must be owner of record before the ex-dividend date. The ex-dividend date is the date on which a stock goes ex-dividend, typically about one to three weeks before the dividend is paid to shareholders of record. Typically, a stock's price moves up by the dollar amount of the dividend as the ex-dividend date approaches, then falls by the amount of the dividend after that date.

Smaller growth companies don't normally pay dividends. They like to keep their earnings to reinvest back into the company for expansion. Reinvesting their earnings helps them avoid going to the bank or to the market to borrow for their future growth.

When a stock's price rises rapidly, some companies choose to split their stock. A *stock split* is a way to reduce a stock's price to a more marketable level for investors. More investors will consider buying a stock that is priced at $30 per share than one priced at $100. One hundred shares at $30 is only $3,000, but 100 shares of the second total $10,000.

If a company decides to split its stock priced at $60 per share at 2 for 1, the 100 shares you presently own ($6,000 worth) are increased to 200 shares. But the value of each share is simultaneously split in half; your net value doesn't change. After the split, you have 200 shares priced at $30 per share; your net value remains at $6,000.

Where Do You Buy Stocks?

You need to buy stocks through a broker. The business of a broker is to find the best price available for the purchase or sale of that stock. Only a broker can execute an order to buy or sell stocks. *Full service brokers* provide research and advice when making investment decisions. *Discount brokers* act strictly as agents for your transactions and do not offer investment advice.

Each time you buy or sell a stock, you pay a *commission*. A portion of that commission goes to your broker. The rest goes to the firm to cover costs associated with the transaction.

Stocks are traded either on an *exchange* (listed) or *over-the-counter* (unlisted). *Listed* means that the stock is listed and traded on a national or regional exchange. These exchanges are organized marketplaces in which members of the exchange trade stocks and bonds. They have physical locations where brokers and dealers meet to execute orders from institutional and individual investors to buy and sell securities. The number of stocks listed on the exchanges is constantly changing because new companies are listed and others can be removed. Stocks may be removed for no longer meeting an exchange's financial standards.

The New York Stock Exchange

The New York Stock Exchange is the oldest and largest. To my knowledge, extended documentation of its history has yet to be written. Some say it started as early as 1725, when the market dealt in commodities such as wheat and tobacco. Others say it began very informally near the time of the birth of our nation when our first Secretary of the Treasury needed to set up a monetary system. One thing seems certain: in both cases, investors are said to have met under a tree at the foot of a street in New York called *Wall*. They eventually moved indoors; from this beginning emerged the New York Stock Exchange.

The New York Stock Exchange (NYSE) accounts for a majority of the business transacted on all organized exchanges in the U.S. The NYSE has the most stringent requirements for companies to meet to be listed on its exchange. It sets its own requirements for membership. The shares of most large companies in the U.S. are publicly traded on the New York Stock Exchange (NYSE). There are thousands of stocks listed on the NYSE.

Let's say you decided to buy 100 shares of Wal-Mart stock. Your order to buy Wal-Mart would be sent via computer to a location on the floor of the NYSE. There, a *specialist* who deals with Wal-Mart stock would receive your order and would then try to match your buy order with a sell order from someone else at a price similar to the previous trade's price.

The Over-the-Counter Market

If you are looking for stocks that are smaller and more risky but may offer you substantial rewards, you might want to shop in the *over-the-counter* (OTC) market. The OTC market tends to be made up of companies that are too small and too new to be listed on the major exchanges.

The main purpose of the OTC market is to provide a market for new issues and secondary issues of unlisted securities, and to facilitate trading in unlisted securities already issued and publicly held. Many great growth issues have emerged from the OTC market over the years: McDonald's, Wendy's, Microsoft and Intel are only a few of the familiar names that started there.

However, the OTC market involves much more than just stocks. It is the market for all transactions which do *not* take place on an exchange. With minor exceptions, this includes all trading in U.S. government and agency securities, money market instruments, municipal bonds, and mutual funds. Corporate bonds also trade frequently in this market. The OTC *stock* market is the best known to investors, however.

The OTC market does not have a physical-trading floor where stocks are traded like the exchanges. Instead, it is an electronic marketplace linked by computers. Market makers or dealers working for brokerage firms keep an inventory of the stock and set buy and sell (bid and offer) prices. These prices are shown on computer screens at dealer firms around the country. This computer system is called NASDAQ – the National Association of Securities Dealers Automated Quote system. It provides quotations from dealers who are willing to buy and sell shares on a continuous basis for their own accounts or for accounts for brokers who phone in with orders.

The NASDAQ listings have an abundant number of small, unnoticed companies, some of which are selling at very low prices. They may be undervalued because too few people have taken a look at their financial statements.

This is not a market for the faint-hearted. Though you may find tomorrow's big winner here, you may well find the future's big loser. The OTC market is typically where the hot stock tips come from. *Beware!* The big winners in this market are those small companies that are major competitors in emerging fields.

Penny stocks are stocks that typically sell for less than $5 per share. They may just be low-priced stocks, but they may also be high-risk stocks or potential rip offs! Many times they rise rapidly right after they start trading, usually because of heavy promotion, possibly because unscrupulous securities firms have manipulated them.

The Securities and Exchange Commission (SEC) has created a rule that requires a broker to determine, in writing, that penny stocks are suitable investments for you. The broker must get detailed financial information and the customer's investment experience before any trade is binding.

The important thing to remember is that you are taking a lot more risk than you would normally take buying mature blue chip stocks. Finally, look for three warning signs of penny-stock fraud: unsolicited phone calls, high-pressure sales tactics, and the inability to sell the stocks and receive cash.

Market Indices

How did the market do today?

That question is usually answered with a reference to the *Dow Jones Industrial Average* (DJIA or the Dow), comprised of 30 stocks listed on the New York Stock Exchange. The Dow is the most widely followed stock market index. The Dow Jones Average is actually made up of four averages – the Industrial, the Composite, the Utility and the Transportation. The best known is the Industrial.

The DJIA (the Dow) was developed back in the late 1880s. Then it was comprised of only 11 stocks. In 1916, the Dow added nine stocks to its average. The Dow was broadened in 1928 to include its present number of 30 stocks. The Dow's 30 stocks are blue-chip companies that represent a significant portion of the market value of stocks listed on the New York Stock Exchange.

The Dow is considered a barometer of the stock market and the economy. The 30 stocks in the Dow are the companies that best represent our economy. Back in the early 1900s, the Dow was made up mostly of industrial companies like steel and railroads. Those companies best represented our economy back then. Today, our economy is made up of more service-type corporations; the Dow reflects that with companies like McDonald's and Wal-Mart who are part of the average.

Who determines which stocks will be in the Dow? The editors of the *Wall Street Journal* decide which stocks will be included. They don't change the stocks very often. They will make a change when they feel a company no longer represents our economy. They generally replace a stock with another in a similar field.

Calculating the Dow Jones Industrial Average is not as simple as adding all 30 stock prices and dividing by 30. The Dow is price-weighted – that is, the total of component stock prices is divided by a divisor. As a result, a high-priced stock has a greater influence on the index than a low-priced stock. This means that one or two stocks can distort the Dow average with significant price fluctuations.

For example, let's say that 29 of the 30 Dow stocks ended the day's trading with just slight increases, while one high-priced stock included in the Dow went down $20 per share. What would that do to the average? It would probably show a down close; people would then assume the market was down. But the overall market was not necessarily down, even though the Dow reflected a down day.

What might give us a better indicator of how the market did today? The *Standard & Poor's* (S&P 500) stock index may give us a better reading (barometer) of the market. The index is made up of 400 industrial, 20 transportation, 40 utility and 40 financial stocks.

The *S&P 500* is a list of stocks that are traded on the NYSE, the American Stock Exchange and the OTC market. However, the index consists primarily of NYSE-listed stocks. Not only is this a broader list of stocks than the Dow; it is a market-weighted index. That means each stock influences the index in proportion to the number of its shares outstanding and the market value of those shares. Because of this, the index cannot be influenced greatly by one or two stocks and that is why many use this index as a barometer to measure the market.

There are many other averages that you can watch to follow the markets. The OTC Index, the Wilshire 5000 Equity Index and the NYSE Composite Index are just a few others that investors like to watch. Investors and traders like to watch more specific indexes, such as the drug, utility, technology or bank stock indexes. These specific indexes measure the value and changes of the stocks in each of their sectors.

How Stocks are Analyzed

Before you buy a stock, the first thing you must do is to decide which one to buy. No problem, right? Well, it all depends on how you go about it. On paper, figuring out which stock to buy can make factual sense ... but facts alone won't guarantee success. The other part of the stock selection process involves consumer psychology and unexpected events.

Unfortunately, we cannot quantify investor psychology or predict the unexpected easily. Some stocks on paper may not look too healthy but, because of investor expectations, the stock may rise for many years. Obviously it's pretty hard to predict unexpected events. Stocks react – most often negatively – to unexpected events, especially world unrest. Because we cannot control psychology or predict future events, we need to use other ways to evaluate stocks.

There are two major schools of thought on picking stocks. Many serious investors swear by *fundamental analysis*. Fundamental analysis involves appraising a company's financial condition and management, as well as its competitive position in its industry.

Other investors live and die by *technical analysis*. Technical analysis ignores fundamentals, instead using charts of past performance to identify price trends and cyclical movements of particular stocks, industries or the market as a whole.

Those who feel every factor must be considered synthesize the two and form an opinion using both methods. Most analysts take into account information from both fundamental and technical analysis when formulating a buy, sell or hold recommendation on a stock.

Fundamental Analysis

Fundamental analysis involves an estimate of the stock's *value* by looking at the basic facts about the company. Once the company's value is determined, it is compared to the stock's current market price. If the stock's market price is lower than the value of the company, analysts recommend purchasing the stock. If the company's value is lower than the current market price of the stock, then typically the investment firm will recommend that you sell the stock.

Critical to fundamental analysis is the evaluation of *earnings* and *book value*. Fundamental analysis also looks at the company's *balance sheet* and *management capability*. In addition, analysts spend a lot of time visiting the companies, talking to them about their prospects for the future.

Much of this information can be found in both Value Line and Standard & Poor's Stock Guide. These publications help simplify some of the analysis to make it easier for investors to understand. These publications can normally be found at brokerage firms or local libraries.

Another place to find financial information is in *research reports* issued by brokerage firms. They are tailored in form so investors can easily read and digest the information. The brokerage firm analyst talks to management and makes a recommendation on the stock based on his or her projections and earnings estimates.

Technical Analysis

Technical analysis involves looking at the past sequence of stock prices. Its concern is with the historical movement of the stock's price. Unlike the fundamentalists who look at companies' value based on earnings, the *technicians* focus on past price patterns and volume figures. They love to use charts.

They use dozens of different techniques to interpret those figures. They record *past prices* and other technical data like *trading volume, moving averages, resistance* and *support levels*, and *advance/decline lines*. They say that stock prices generally tend to move in trends that persist for significant periods of time. They maintain that chart patterns often tend to recur. These recurring patterns can be used to forecast future prices.

How To Buy Stocks

Once you've made the decision about which stock or stocks to buy, you must then decide on a method to purchase them. While there are a large number of sophisticated ways to buy stocks, we'll look at a few of the strategies that the average investor should understand.

If you've found tomorrow's winner, are ready to buy it, and are willing to pay the current market price, you will enter a market order. A *market order* requires you to accept the current price of the stock when the order reaches the trading floor. Most orders executed on the exchanges are market orders. If you've decided to buy a stock, you normally enter a market order to buy the stock.

If you want to buy or sell a particular stock but aren't willing to buy or sell it at the current market price, then you can enter a limit order. A *limit order* means that you have placed an order to buy or sell a stock at a specified price. The order won't fill until the stock reaches the price you specified in the limit order.

For example, let's say you want to buy Coke at a stock price of $30, assuming it is trading at $33. You could put in a limit order to buy Coke at $30. This means that your order will not fill unless Coke stock traded down to at least $30 per share.

On the other hand, if you put in a limit order to sell at $35, your stock will not sell unless the stock price reaches or exceeds $35 per share. If it doesn't reach $35, your sell order will not execute.

If you want your order to be in effect for only one day, you can use a *day order*; your order will be in effect for only one day. If you feel sure the stock's price is going to meet your price expectations, you can also enter an *open order*, or *good-'til-cancelled order*. This type of order gives permission to execute your open order at any later date if the price of the stock should return to your limit price.

One way to help reduce losing money in a particular stock is by using a *stop order*. A stop order is an order to sell at a specified price, called the stop price.

A stop order to sell, always at a price below the current market price, is usually designed to protect a profit or to limit a loss on a security already purchased at a higher price. The risk of stop orders is that they may be triggered by a temporary market movement or be executed at prices lower than the stop price because of market orders ahead of them.

Foreign Stocks – Why Invest Internationally?

As the economy becomes increasingly global in nature, more and more people are investing in foreign companies. ***The biggest reason to invest internationally is to buy the great companies overseas.*** This is the best way to take advantage of those companies who are going to profit from rapidly developing countries.

Another reason for investing abroad is *diversification*. Markets in different countries don't always move in sync. International diversification can help investors enhance their returns. For example in 1993, the Dow Jones Industrial Average rose 10%. If an investor had a portion of his or her portfolio in a mutual fund that buys the big companies overseas, he or she would have earned around 35% on the international portion of the portfolio. This would have increased the overall return of the portfolio significantly.

Many of the world's leading corporations are based overseas, including:

> 7 of the 10 largest banks
> 8 of the 10 largest electrical and electronics firms
> 5 of the 10 largest broadcasting and publishing companies
> 9 of the 10 largest construction and housing companies

Capitalism is exploding in places where it was unknown just a decade ago. Thousands of companies have been created over the past ten years by privatizing state-run services such as airlines, telephone companies and banks. Rising standards of living are accelerating demand for goods and services around the world.

Every day, you use products or services from companies based outside the United States. Consider these common brand names:

Brand	**Company**	**Country**
Close-Up	Unilever	Netherlands
Dannon	Groupe Danone	France
Eureka	Electrolux	Sweden
Mott's	Cadbury Schweppes	United Kingdom
7-Eleven	Ito-Yokado	Japan
Shell	Royal Dutch Petroleum	Netherlands
Travelodge	Forte	United Kingdom

If you are interested in investing in foreign individual stocks, you can buy into the companies in the form of American Depository Receipts, or ADRs. *ADRs* are a receipt for the shares of a foreign-based corporation held in the vault of a U.S. bank and entitling the shareholder to all dividends and capital gains. One of the features of owning ADRs is that the bank eliminates many of the inconveniences involved in owning foreign shares, including issuing dividends in American dollars and handling such matters as stock splits. ADRs generally trade over-the-counter, though a few are listed on the New York Stock Exchange.

One of the greatest risks involved in foreign securities ownership is the currency risk. Foreign currency fluctuations may cut into any stock gains you may have. Additionally, it is many times harder to evaluate foreign companies because of different accounting standards.

To eliminate these potential problems, you most often would be best off buying stocks of foreign companies through mutual funds that specialize in foreign investing.

Chapter 4: Mutual Funds

How many hours of sleep have you lost wondering what is going to happen to the stock you recently purchased…when the quote in today's paper showed that it went down 50%? How many nights have you lain awake second-guessing your decision to buy or sell stock? When should I buy? When should I sell? Are they going bankrupt? Will I lose my money?

Questions like these are normal. If these kinds of decisions make you uncomfortable, an alternative choice for your savings might be to invest in a *mutual fund*. This type of professional money management allows you to own different types of investments while reducing risk through diversification.

What is professional management? Professional money management is nothing more than a fund manager who takes the money you've invested and makes buy-and-sell decisions on your behalf. Most money managers work for mutual fund companies.

There are two ways to invest your money with professional money managers. One is by investing in a managed account where the money managers require a minimum of $100,000. These money managers do not charge a fee initially when you put your money in or when you take it out. Rather, you pay as you go. The money managers typically charge a management fee ranging from 1% to 3% of the portfolio's total assets each year.

The other way to attain professional money management is by investing in a mutual fund. With as little as $250, or less in some cases, you can invest your savings with the same kind of diversification and money management with a lot less money. With a mutual fund, you have the same access to money management as do people with larger sums of money.

Mutual Funds

Purchasing a mutual fund is an excellent alternative for investors who lack the time or expertise to manage their own diversified portfolio of investments. A mutual fund is simply a way for many people with different amounts of available cash to pool their money to gain professional management in exchange for a fee.

For example, let's say you have $10,000 to invest and want to buy stocks for growth. Alone, with $10,000, you cannot obtain proper diversification with individual common stocks. Moreover, by buying individual stocks, you would need to make your own buy-and-sell decisions.

But let's say that there are also 99 other people in a similar situation with $10,000 to invest. If you and the other 99 people pool your money, together you have $1 million. With that $1 million, you'd have enough money to spread yourself properly among different stocks and industries. You'd also be able to hire some of the best money managers to monitor your investments.

That's what a mutual fund is. It's simply pooling your money with funds from other people with similar goals, then giving that money to a professional money manager who will properly diversify your holdings.

A mutual fund can encompass almost any kind of investment. For example, if a mutual fund has 200 stocks in it, your $10,000 includes ownership of a small piece of every one of the 200 companies. If something happened to one of the 200 companies in the fund, it wouldn't affect your money much. Remember, 199 other companies are holding up the value of your mutual fund.

The mutual fund industry has been around for a long time. The first mutual fund in the U.S. was created back in the early 1920s, but the concept didn't really take off until the 1970s. It virtually exploded throughout the 1980s and 1990s. In response to this demand for professional money management, there are now more than 8,000 mutual funds. They cover many different objectives and risk levels. Some mutual funds specialize in mature blue chip stocks; others in riskier, fast-growing companies. Some funds emphasize income while others aim for growth.

Specialized funds allow you to concentrate on specific areas of the economy. Some funds emphasize short-term money markets; others own long-term bonds. There are about as many different fund-objective categories as there are days in the month. The important thing is to find the right balance of funds to meet your specific goals.

Types of Mutual Funds

Open-end mutual funds are by far the most popular type of mutual fund. These funds can issue an unlimited number of shares so their *size will change* as people send in money to invest or take money out. If a great many people one day decide to add money to their fund, they'd send their cash to the fund, where the money manager would take that money and use it to add to the size of the fund.

Conversely, if a number of people decided simultaneously to sell some of their mutual fund, the mutual fund company would sell some of the shares of that fund, thereby making its size smaller, with fewer shares outstanding. Thus, the number of shares held by the fund continuously increases or decreases based directly on share purchases and redemptions. Most mutual funds that you read about are typically the *open-end* mutual funds.

Closed-end mutual funds have a *fixed*, limited number of shares out-standing. When you purchase shares in a closed-end fund, the seller is a fellow investor, rather than the fund itself as with open-end funds. When you sell shares of your closed-end fund, the buyer is another investor and not the fund.

The closed-end fund shares trade on an exchange or over-the-counter as a stock does. You can purchase these funds through your broker who will charge you a commission that is roughly standard for any listed security.

What is the purpose of closed-end funds? Generally, these funds are created with a specific focus such as a portfolio that holds government, tax-free, junk bonds or a certain group of stocks. The hope is that these particular securities in the closed-end funds will outperform similar ones in open-end funds. The one charac-teristic that separates them from the open-end funds is their prices will change not only by the securities' underlying value, but also by the supply and demand for the particular fund.

How a Mutual Fund Works

A mutual fund can make money for investors in several ways. One is through dividends and interest earned on its investments. The divi-dends and interest are passed on to the shareholders. They are treated as taxable income for that year, just as any interest from other invest-ments would be. The earnings can be paid monthly or quarterly, de-pending on which type of mutual fund you own.

If the mutual fund manager decides to sell an investment within the fund for a profit, the profit would be passed on to you in the form of a capital gain. A capital gain is the profit of the security sold within the fund. These gains are usually paid semi-annually or annually.

You don't have to take dividends, interest and capital gains in cash. In fact, unless you really need the money, I recommend investors reinvest any distributions received to purchase additional shares of the fund. This can be done very easily by indicating on the account application that you wish to reinvest all dividends and capital gains. Additionally, most funds allow you to reinvest these dividends and capital gains without paying a fee on the reinvested shares.

Help or No-Help?

Much is made of whether investors should pay a fee to an advisor or not to invest their money. The answer is very simple. If you need *help* investing your money you should pay an advisor a fee to help you manage your finances. If you don't have time to do research and become knowledgeable in investments and other financial planning issues, and are busy with your own children, business and social life, it makes sense to pay an advisor to help you manage your financial future.

Let's look at the difference between **Help** (load) and **No-Help** (no-load) funds.

Help funds are funds that your financial advisor builds into a life-long investment strategy. In exchange for a fee, your advisor makes recommendations on which mutual funds to buy to help you reach your goals. These mutual funds are sometimes referred to as load funds.

No-Help funds are funds that you buy without help or advice. You, on your own, make all investment planning decisions. You do not get the benefit of an advisor's recommendations. These funds are sometimes referred to as no-load funds.

In the end, one type of fund (Help or No-Help) is not better than the other, they are just different. With a Help fund you get advice and with No-Help you don't get advice. Do you need advice to do your life-long investment planning? Your answer will determine which type of fund is best for you.

Help Mutual Funds

Help mutual funds charge a fee for purchasing shares. This fee is paid to the financial advisor for his or her advice. There are many ways that mutual funds can charge fees. The following three fee structures are the most common:

The most common fee structure for help funds is the fee that is paid *up-front*. Most help funds have a fee ranging from 3% to 5 3/4%. Generally, once you have paid your initial fee, there will be no additional fees when you sell the fund. From the fee that you pay when you buy the fund, the financial advisor gets a portion as compensation for his or her advice. In the newspaper, this fee is reflected in the difference between the net asset value (NAV) and the public offering price (POP). Generally, the funds that charge an up-front fee are considered class **'A'** shares.

Some funds charge no fees when you buy, but may charge a fee when you sell, depending on the length of time you hold the fund. Generally the amount of the fee will decline as you hold the fund shares for a longer period of time. This is called a redemption fee (back-end fee) and considered class **'B'** shares.

Eventually (usually after five years) you can sell the fund without a back-end (selling) fee. The fee that the advisor receives from this type of fund is taken out of the fund as an expense on an annual basis. Generally, an *additional one percent annual fee* is added to the fund's total operating expenses to compensate for the advisor's fee. This additional one percent annual fee normally lasts from four to six years and then is eliminated.

Finally, the third basic fee structure for help mutual funds is the class **'C'** shares. With this type of fee structure, the investor pays a one percent annual fee to the advisor for advice and service. There are, generally, no fees to sell the fund. Investors simply pay as they go - one percent of assets annually. Some investors prefer this type of fee structure because they get the benefit of advice from a trusted financial advisor while compensating the advisor based on the total value of assets being managed. The more rapidly the account grows for the client, the more fees the advisor earns and visa versa.

No-Help Mutual Funds

Generally, No-Help (no-load) mutual funds do not have an up-front fee or additional annual advisor's fee. This can be an advantage in that you can have more money working for you initially in the mutual fund. You do not pay a fee to buy or sell shares in these funds because you do not get any advice making your investment decisions. No-Help mutual funds make money by charging their shareholders *annual management fees* for managing their money.

No-Help mutual funds are sold directly through the mail and through newspaper, radio, television or internet advertising. You will not have the help of a financial advisor in choosing the mutual funds that are best suited for your needs. You, on your own, must select the professional money managers, monitor the fund's performance, time your buys and sells, and make sure the fund is meeting your original objectives. All decisions rest in your hands. That is why they are called no-help funds - you get no advice.

The Help & No-Help Issue

Fees need to be put into proper context for evaluation. On one hand, they impact short-term returns to investors. If his or her investment goal is less than three-to-four years, an investor may be better off considering funds with no up-front or back-end fees.

Importantly, however, the investor must be confident enough to make his or her own market timing and investment decisions. In addition, most people whose investment goal is less than three-to-four years should consider investments like CDs or money markets whose principal doesn't fluctuate – especially when the short-term need is for a specific purpose. That way, you don't have to worry about a bear market that could make your principal decline significantly – especially at the time you need the money most.

On the other hand, fees represent a payment for advisory services. Fees are well-spent money for investors who receive good investment advice. Remember, when you pay a fee to an advisor you are working with that person to establish a life-long investment strategy. The advisor will help you make informed long-term financial planning decisions.

Which is better for you? - **IT DEPENDS**

If you have the time, expertise, resources and ability to sleep while making these decisions without second-guessing yourself and enjoy picking your own group of mutual funds out of more than 8,000 available, then perhaps a no-help fund is appropriate.

If, however, you need help finding the funds that will diversify your assets for the rest of your life and don't have the time, expertise or resources to do your own homework and feel you need an advisor to help you with your investment planning, then a help fund is the perfect answer. If you feel you need investment counsel, it makes sense to buy a help fund.

Internal Fees and Expenses

All mutual funds, whether they're help or no-help, charge *internal management fees*. These fees cover a variety of expenses such as the portfolio manager's salary. It also covers research, mailings, statements and, of course, the advertisements you see in magazines and on the radio and TV. These internal management fees normally range anywhere from $1/2$% to 2% annually, depending on the fund's objective. There may also be a fee that pays for advertising and marketing expenses - it is called a 12-b 1 fee. The 12-b 1 fee is normally included within the fund's reported annual management expenses.

Mutual funds that are more aggressive in buying and selling, such as growth mutual funds, naturally have higher management expenses than those that invest in bonds.

When purchasing a mutual fund, watch to make sure that the fund's management expenses are in line with others in its own category. Some funds charge excessive fees to pay for advertising and other related costs. These excessive fees ultimately eat into the fund's annual profits. *Studies show that funds with lower management fees generally outperform funds with higher management fees over the long-term.* The management fee isn't the only variable to look at, but is one that should be considered when analyzing different funds.

One place these fees can be found is in the mutual fund's *prospectus*. A prospectus is a legal document that describes the fund's objective, its management, its charges and expenses and other essential data.

What to Look for in Mutual Funds

One of the things you must look for in mutual funds is *their performance relative to other funds with the same objective.* One cannot simply say, "Because I earned 12% a year for the last ten years, I had a good mutual fund." If you earned 12% a year during the decade of the 1980's or 90's, you underperformed the stock fund averages. You should have earned significantly more. Twelve percent per year is good only if the other funds in the same category did 12% or less per year.

Without doing a mutual fund evaluation, you cannot be sure if the fund you own or are about to buy is doing well relative to others within its own category. Earning 12% a year sounds good until you find out that the fund's peers returned 17% per year with the same investment objective and fluctuation level!

One the other side of the coin, don't feel bad if one of your funds didn't do as well as your neighbor's. One reason your neighbor's fund may have outperformed yours may be that his or her fund has a higher fluctuation level or had a different investment objective. You may have owned a conservative growth-and-income fund that averaged thirteen percent per year. This may have been right in line with expectations, while your neighbor averaged fifteen percent per year with a more aggressive growth mutual fund. That's reasonable - the more aggressive fund has a higher fluctuation level and should have a higher return. It's not fair to compare the two. *You should only compare your fund with other funds that have the same objective and fluctuation level.*

Because many funds look alike and are similar within their own objective, it is important to find a fund that has superior management. For example, most growth funds own many of the same stocks. So what separates one fund from the other? In other words, if most funds generally own the same stocks, how could one fund consistently outperform another over time? *Management performance.*

Management performance is arguably the most important single variable determining which fund performs the most consistently year after year. Some funds use a star management style where one person calls the shots. Other funds use committee or team style management where a number of people together make decisions on behalf of the fund.

One way to determine a manager's style is to look at the portfolio turnover. The turnover ratio will tell you how often the investments within the fund are being bought and sold in one year. Does the fund have a high turnover, or is management using a buy-and-hold strategy with low turnover? Does the fund have high or low internal expenses? Generally, *studies show that mutual funds with below-average turnover and internal management fees perform better than those with higher turnover and management expenses.*

Internal expenses, turnover ratio and management structure all contribute to defining the fund's management style. As an Investor-for-Life (IFL), it is very important that you find a style that you understand and are comfortable with. *Consistency through good and bad markets is the key!*

When looking at mutual funds, one of the things you want to avoid is choosing the hottest or best fund of the moment. Funds that do spectacularly well when the market is rising often do spectacularly poorly when it begins to fall. It is wise to look for funds that have been consistently profitable over the years, those that have performed well in both up and down markets. This provides the best test of fund managers' ability to handle money over the long-term.

Benefits of Mutual Funds

One important benefit of mutual funds is *diversification*. Diversification allows you to spread your fluctuation risk among different investments. One question many investors have is, "Can I lose all my money in a well-diversified mutual fund?" Well, let's say you owned a mutual fund that has 200 stocks in its portfolio and *one* of the 200 companies within the fund went bankrupt. It really isn't going to affect your investment very much because your fund has 199 other stocks holding up its value. If, however, you had put all your money in one stock, the one that went bankrupt, you would have lost all your money.

Another benefit is *convenience*. Some mutual funds allow investors to start out with a minimum investment as small as $100. This gives investors with small amounts of money to invest the ability to take advantage of the same kind of investments as people with larger amounts. In addition, you normally have the privilege of automatically reinvesting both dividends and capital gains without fees. This enables you to speed up your compounding potential and eliminates your decision on what to do with the dividend checks.

Having professionals do your *record-keeping* is a tremendous benefit of mutual funds. You have the choice of taking the dividends or capital gains in cash or reinvesting them. You simply make your choice when you open the account; the fund takes care of the rest. At the end of the year, the fund will provide you with a year-end summary of all transactions. Additionally, at year-end the fund will provide you with tax information regarding your distributions.

Investing in mutual funds allows you to do all the things you want, without the worry of making buy and sell decisions. Instead of staying home analyzing your investments, losing sleep, or wondering if you are going to lose your money, you can be out golfing, playing with your children or grandchildren, getting a suntan at the lake or enjoying life fishing.

Chapter 5: Diversification for the Traditional Investor

One of the key financial goals for *traditional investors* is to achieve good long-term returns with as little fluctuation as possible. Reducing fluctuation can help investors feel more comfortable in the investment process.

To achieve reduced fluctuation via traditional diversification, most investors normally allocate their money among the four basic types of assets: stocks, bonds, CDs, and money market. One would ordinarily make allocation decisions to each of the categories based on age and goals.

Unlike diversification for the IFLs (Investors-for-Life), who are more interested in diversifying into stocks to achieve long-term rising income with annual returns in the 11% range, *traditional investors prefer diversification that will reduce fluctuation*. The traditional investor is comfortable achieving annual returns of around 6 ½ to 7% per year (45% stocks, 45% bonds & CDs, 10% money market) in return for the reduced fluctuation.

The Advantage of Traditional Diversification is Threefold

First, asset allocation allows you to take advantage of many investment opportunities among one or any of the asset categories as their prices become good relative values.

Second, asset allocation prevents you from putting all your eggs in one basket, thereby reducing the level of fluctuation in any given period.

Third, it allows you to maximize your returns relative to your tolerance for fluctuation.

Take Advantage of Current Economic Conditions

One of the advantages of traditional diversification is that investors are allocating their money among any or all four basic types of assets. A traditional investor's portfolio might have allocated some money in stocks, bonds, CDs, and money market.

Economic trends change over time. For example, there are times when interest rates are high. This can be a good period to purchase bonds and CDs because you can lock in a high rate of interest for a fixed period of time. These high interest rates will look really attractive when the economy slows down and interest rates fall.

There are times when stocks look more attractive than other assets. For example, during an extended recession (bear market), common stock prices normally decline to unusually attractive values. These temporary declines offer investors an excellent opportunity to buy shares in some great companies at very low prices. Eventually, as the stock market returns to its permanent rise, investors who purchased these stocks when they were temporarily down will be rewarded greatly in the form of above average returns in the future.

As interest rates rise and fall, your portfolio can take advantage of interest rates as they are offered. If interest rates rise above normal, investors can take advantage of the temporary rise by locking in the attractive rates for longer periods of time, thereby increasing the overall future returns for their portfolio.

By having a number of different types of investments, investors can have more opportunities to take advantage of the continually changing economic environment. Because of the cyclical nature of the economy, investors can normally take advantage of short-term anomalies as they present themselves.

Reduce Fluctuation

One of the biggest benefits of diversification among different asset categories is a *reduction in portfolio fluctuation*. Reduced fluctuation is the most often used concept that investors and advisors rely on when constructing a diversified portfolio for traditional investors.

To give you an example, a traditionally diversified portfolio which includes stocks, bonds, CDs and money market will fluctuate less than a portfolio that includes only stocks. An all-stock portfolio has the potential to decline 25% or more in a short period of time. On the other hand, a traditionally diversified portfolio would more likely decline much less in a period where stocks are down 25%. A diversified portfolio might decline more in the neighborhood of around 10 to 15% in a down period.

By allocating some of your money in bonds, CDs and money market with stocks, you can achieve long-term returns that will provide you with less fluctuation than an all-stock portfolio.

Maximize Returns Relative To Your Tolerance for Fluctuation

For the traditional investor, there are two basic variables that will have an effect on how your portfolio is allocated: *age* and *fluctuation comfort level*. Every person's financial situation is different. Each has a different approach to asset allocation, allowing for more fluctuation to less fluctuation.

Your age and goals have a direct affect on how your assets may be allocated. The less time you have to accomplish your investment objective, the less fluctuation you would want. If you know little Grant is going to need money for college in a few years, you don't want to do anything that would jeopardize his education. If, however, your money were earmarked for retirement 30 years from now, you'd be wise to allocate a larger percentage of your money to stocks to get more growth.

Second, investors need to be able to sleep at night! All the rules, investment books and counsel you receive from your financial advisors are worthless unless you can live with the level of fluctuation your portfolio is producing. If you are an investor who is willing to give up some upside return for less fluctuation, by all means take the route of investing that will meet your psychological needs.

Allocating Your Money by Percentages

The next step is to quantify all those things that go into your allocation makeup with your financial advisor. After determining your tolerance for fluctuation, picking the time horizon and establishing your goals, you will need to put a certain amount of money in each of the four investment areas: stocks, bonds, CDs and money market. You will then allocate money based on percentages in each investment area that will fulfill your needs.

Remember that there are no hard and fast rules that state the proportion of your money that should be in any one area. The percentages allocated to each area are relative to your own personal needs.

Two different traditional investor's portfolios might look something like this:

	Common Stocks	Bonds	CDs	Money Market
35-year-old	80%	10%	5%	5%
65-year-old	50%	20%	20%	10%

As you can see, the 35-year-old investor has more time to prepare for retirement needs, so his or her investment portfolio will require a higher percentage of its total money to be allocated in growth investments and less in the fixed income area.

The traditional 65-year-old investor, however, may have different needs. More specifically, he or she may want more current fixed income to live on while minimizing principal fluctuation. Then, more money could be allocated to the fixed income areas such as bonds and CDs.

You'll notice that the allocation example has some of its money allocated to common stocks for both investors. Unless you have more money than you will ever need, most investors have to worry about the rising cost of living and will need at least some of their money growing faster than inflation and taxes. Over the long-term, more reliably than any other investment, stocks have outpaced inflation and taxes and have allowed investors to increase their standard of living with age.

Once you've figured out how much money you are going to allocate in each of the investment areas to achieve proper diversification for your needs, you are going to need a system to monitor your portfolio. Your advisor should have in place a portfolio analysis that together you can review periodically to see how the different investments are doing.

This portfolio analysis should report exactly how each of the investments is doing since you've begun investing. Additionally, it should be able to show you how your allocation percentages have changed due to your investments' performance. This will allow you to make changes and re-allocate as economic conditions change. It is important that you monitor how your portfolio is doing periodically.

Final Thoughts on Diversification for the Traditional Investor

When doing a personal asset allocation analysis, be sure to include *all of your estate.* This includes savings and checking accounts, all brokerage accounts, bank accounts (CDs & EE bonds) and importantly, your retirement savings like IRAs, annuities and retirement plans at work. As you build a portfolio that meets your needs and objectives, incorporate your retirement plans into your overall financial picture. To maximize diversification one needs to include all of one's assets.

How often do asset allocation changes need to be made? It depends on how often and to what degree economic conditions change. Review your situation if economic conditions change rapidly. Regardless of economic conditions, be sure to *review your financial situation at least once a year.* This review can be fairly simple. A report should be generated showing how each of your investments has done in the past period and where your current allocations stand. If your allocation percentages are off by 10% or more in a particular asset category, you might consider making allocation changes.

The most appealing attribute of traditional diversification is reduced overall portfolio fluctuation. By incorporating bonds and CDs into a great stock portfolio, investors will reduce some temporary downward portfolio fluctuation. If interest rates rise to a level above historical means (like 9% +), investing in bonds and CDs can make a diversified portfolio perform very well over a period of time. It is in high interest rate times when the traditionally diversified portfolio looks most attractive and is most effective.

Chapter 6: Re-Defining 'Risk'

Don't Run Out of Money Before Running Out of Life

Risk is one of the most widely used concepts investors use to determine whether or not to buy an investment. Unfortunately, many investors' definition of risk may not be exactly accurate, depending on the person's understanding of what risk really is.

For many people, the basic understanding of 'risk' and 'safety' comes from the Great Depression – a massive period of deflation during which most lost their principal. It didn't matter whether one was an investor in New York City who owned a piece of Fifth Avenue and a portfolio of common stocks or a farmer in the Midwest who owned farmland, machinery and common stock mutual funds - at the Depression's end, the value of most things had gone down. This loss of principal is the understanding of risk that, if we didn't experience it directly, our parents and grandparents taught us.

How do you define *risk*? Most people define risk simply as losing their money. While I don't disagree that people could lose all their money if they put it in a bad stock or bond, intelligent investors would not put all their money in just one company's stock. If investors were to put their money into a mutual fund that owned 1,000 of the world's greatest companies, you could confidently say that the risk of losing all their money is impossible. By diversifying into a large number of stocks, investors can eliminate the risk of losing all their money. Consequently, one can eliminate the 'old' definition of risk.

Yes, temporary principal declines are a risk, and a fluctuation risk is not to be taken lightly. But have you ever considered that there might be another risk in your life - even more real than the risk of watching one's principal decline temporarily? *How about the risk that your retirement income won't keep up with the rising costs of living for the rest of your life.* As we retire much sooner and live a lot longer, even very low levels of inflation are going to turn our dollars into pennies over time. In 1972 a stamp cost 6 cents; by 1995 that same stamp costs 32 cents. The longer you live, the bigger this risk becomes.

How do you define *safety*? Most people would respond with just the opposite of risk - keeping one's principal safe. But safe from what? Safe from the rising costs of living? It is very easy to keep your principal from fluctuating by buying CDs. But because your principal and income can never grow, you have exposed your money, in my opinion, to the greatest financial risk of all - erosion of purchasing power. With fixed income investments like CDs and bonds, you can only get back, at maturity, what you put in. But, because of the rising costs of living, what you put in five or ten years ago will not buy as much ten or 20 years in the future. *In the real world of persistent inflation, putting all your money in fixed income investments is not very safe at all.*

Thirty years ago, our parents or grandparents often retired at 65 and died at 72. Risk means something different today than it did in the past. Today, people are living much longer. The average person is living a quarter of a century *after* retirement, and he or she continues to invest in fixed income investments like CDs and Government bonds whose principal and interest never grow. This obsession with principal can be financially devastating to people.

In the first half of the 20th century, most people worked for a company until retirement, then lived off their retirement savings until death. Their life expectancy was significantly shorter than today's. People were able to take their retirement savings and live off the income until they died. Life expectancy was shorter so they required less money to live. The rising costs of living didn't affect as many people back then.

Today, things are different. We are living much longer into our retirement years. The average 60-year-old has a life expectancy of an additional 21 years. It is normal today to see people living 20 to 30 years or more in retirement! It is easy to see that if a person needs to live off his or her retirement savings, that income is going to need to grow for a long, long time. Inflation, or the rising cost of living, is a big threat for today's and tomorrow's retirees.

Risk has changed because life has changed. Not only are people living longer, but since the Great Depression, our country has not seen another decade in which prices have fallen. During every decade since the Depression, the costs of the things we buy have gone up.

 The primary risk for people today, and in the 21st century, is erosion of purchasing power; that is, outliving one's income. I don't mean literally running out of money, although that is a possibility. I mean the risk of the income one lives on from year-to-year not keeping up with the perpetual rise in the cost of the goods and services a person buys.

Let's say someone is getting a fixed income of $3,000 a month from his or her CDs, bonds, and other savings. Sounds ok today, right? How about getting $3,000 a month for the next 21 years? Remember, the costs of the things you buy are going to go up virtually every year. If your income doesn't rise along with prices, you may eventually outlive your fixed retirement income. Remember the cost of the stamp 20 years ago?

Someone might ask himself, "Will $36,000 a year today buy as many things as $36,000 a year ten or 20 years from now?" Obviously not! For example, with an average annual inflation rate of 3 ½ % for the next 21 years, that $36,000 annual income 21 years from now would be worth about $18,000 in today's dollars. Assuming one is used to living on $36,000 annually, he must ask himself, "Can I afford to cut my income in half?" If the answer is "no" and you can't afford to live on less, then it is important that you get your income to go up for the *rest of your life* to keep up with the rising cost of living.

How can one achieve rising income to offset the increasing cost of living? One way is by receiving the dividends that the great companies in America and around the world pay on their common stocks. Many of these companies have been raising the dividends they pay for many, many years. One of the most convenient ways to own those great businesses is by buying good quality mutual funds or variable annuities with a long track record of rising dividends. Investments like these should help keep one's income rising throughout one's life.

Fluctuation Is NOT Loss

What do most people like least about owning a portfolio of common stocks? The *fluctuation*! This is the attribute that keeps many people from owning and staying with this great investment.

Fluctuation is not loss; unless you choose to make it so with a panicky sell decision. The value of the shares of the great companies in the U.S. and around the world is going to fluctuate - up mostly, but never mind that. Every once in a while their share prices will go down temporarily. But they never stay down. Every time the stock market went down it ultimately recovered and moved on to new highs.

All investments have a **cost** and a **benefit**. In *savings* (CDs, Treasury bills, savings accounts, money markets) the benefit is you know exactly how many dollars you have today and how many you will have tomorrow. Your principal stays virtually constant all the time. There is great comfort in this.

The *cost* of the emotional comfort in *savings* is that the returns are almost always negative after factoring in taxes and inflation. In other words, your dollars are losing value relative to what you can buy with that money. The price of everything you need to live on is constantly rising and that means that the value of your dollars is declining.

In *investing* (common stocks), your money has a different cost and benefit. The *cost* of investing is that the principal is going to fluctuate, mostly upward. The Dow Jones Industrial Average touched 40 in 1932; in 1998 it passed 9,000! I can assure you that there were many periods of time during which the market declined during those years. Some of those periods lasted longer than others. But the share prices of those companies *never stayed down*. The declines have always been temporary.

The *benefit* of investing is that your money, over time, will likely keep ahead of inflation and taxes. No other investment has more reliably provided investors with positive real rates of return than common stocks and the dividends they pay. The cost of this benefit is temporary - it's fluctuation. *And fluctuation is not loss - it's fluctuation.* The *benefit is permanent*; over time, your money and income will grow faster than the rising costs of living.

Remember, risk is not just loss of principal. That's just one risk, and can never again be the only risk. Another risk for people today and in the future, perhaps more important, is loss of purchasing power. You cannot afford to run out of money during your lifetime!

Chapter 7: Rx for Risk: Rising Income

Dividend Growth

One of my beliefs for investing into the next century is that the biggest risk people will face in their financial future is *not* losing their money but **outliving** it. I believe that outliving one's income needs is the greatest single financial risk people will face from here into the 21st century. Unlike our parents and grandparents who lived a shorter lifespan, people today, and in the future, will likely be living another 25 to 30 years **in** their retirement.

Not only will retirees need income for a long, long time; they will also need *income that goes up* during their retirement. The cost of living has gone up every decade since the Great Depression. If your income doesn't rise with the increasing costs of living (food, medical etc.), your standard of living will be declining. Remember that six-cent stamp in 1972? In 1998, that same stamp costs 32 cents. Has your income risen from six cents to 32 cents over the last 26 years?

People who plan for 25 to 30 years of retirement should have as an investment goal not *growth* or *income* but *growth of income*. Historically, no income stream has grown more steadily and reliably than the dividends that the great companies in the U.S. and around the world pay. If you believe that most companies like Coca-Cola, 3M, GE, McDonald's, Campbell Soup Co., Mobil Oil and others will continue to sell their products and make money over time, then you should feel very comfortable with the dividends these companies will pay in the future.

Defining Dividends (The Great Inflation Killer)

Dividends are to stocks what interest is to bonds. The payment you earn from a stock is called a dividend. A *dividend* is a payment of cash to the shareholder of a common stock of a company. As companies make money, they can pay out some of their earnings in the form of a dividend to the shareholder.

Not all companies pay a dividend. The companies that normally pay dividends are the more mature, well-known type. Smaller or fast-growing companies normally retain their earnings so they can expand and make their company grow without having to borrow even more money from banks and others.

Let me give you a simplified example of how and where a dividend comes from. Let's assume company X makes $1 million dollars in earnings this year. Let's also assume that there are one million shares of common stock held by investors. That means there was a $1 profit for each share (one million shares) – right? Right. So if a company were to be prudent, it wouldn't want to pay out all of its profits to the share-holders. It may need some of that money to pay for expenses and unex-pected emergencies. So most companies choose to retain some of their earnings each year.

Conversely, why don't some companies retain all of their earnings? Many companies don't need all that money to run their businesses. If they aren't expanding as rapidly as in the past, they can choose to reward the shareholders of the company in the form of the dividend.

Let's say that company X will retain 50% of its earnings and pay out 50% in the form of a cash dividend; it will keep those percentages fixed each year. Since company X has one million shares and $1 million in earnings, each share had earnings of $1. So what would be the dividend for each share? Right! Fifty cents per share (50% of $1). So if you owned 1,000 shares, your dividend would be $500 (1,000 shares x 50 cents).

Now, here is where the rising income comes in. Let's assume that company X makes $1,200,000 next year. What would happen to your dividend income next year? Well, if the company's payout ratio stays the same at 50/50, then 50% of $1,200,000 is $600,000. If you still own 1,000 shares of company X, your dividend income would be $600. As these companies' earnings increase, shareholders are rewarded for their patience and long term perspective. The form of that reward: increased dividends, the ultimate inflation killer.

But that's not the whole story. If a company keeps increasing its earnings year after year, and its dividends keep growing along with earnings, it just makes sense that the price of the shares of that company would eventually go up as well. Why? Because the shares become more valuable as the dividend rises.

It is impossible for the price of a stock and the dividend to go in opposite directions for any length of time. Dividend growth signals, in the most concrete way, that a company is doing progressively better. If the company is doing better over time, the price of the stock may go down temporarily once in a while, but it cannot stay down. Ultimately the value of the shares will rise. So, not only can you achieve rising income, but your principal can grow also.

Let's take a look at a case for rising income - Coca-Cola Co. A $10,000 investment in its stock at the end of 1987 would have purchased 2,098 shares, adjusted for splits. Each share paid a dividend of .15 cents in 1988. The income from these shares was $315 (2,098 x .15) in 1988, for a yield of 3.15%.

The following chart illustrates how Coca-Cola's dividend income has grown over the past ten years. Keep in mind, the income in this illustration is shown as being *paid out* to the shareholder to use to live on, pay bills, etc. The share value (principal) is growing *without* dividends being reinvested.

Coca-Cola Co.

Year	Dividend per share	Income paid out	Yield on original investment	Principal value
1988	$.15	$315	3.15%	$11,702
1989	.17	357	3.57	20,259
1990	.20	420	4.20	24,389
1991	.24	504	5.04	42,091
1992	.28	587	5.87	43,927
1993	.34	713	7.13	46,812
1994	.39	818	8.18	54,024
1995	.44	923	9.23	77,888
1996	.50	1,049	10.49	110,407
1997	.56	1,175	11.75	139,910

As you can see, in the ten-year period ending 1997, Coca-Cola paid a very consistent rising dividend that ultimately offset the increasing costs of living. Not only did the income rise consistently, but the share value grew as well. Remember the income was not reinvested. As Coca-Cola's dividend rose over the years, their shares became more valuable and their share price increased as well. Long-term dividend growth is a sure sign that a company is doing progressively better and over time the price of the shares of that company will go up.

Many other companies such as Bristol Meyers, Campbell Soup, Fannie Mae, Gillette, Sara Lee and others have paid rising income via their dividends over the years. Historically, owning these great companies has been the only way to keep your principal and income growing faster than inflation and taxes. It makes sense that most people should have some of their money in these types of companies to achieve rising income.

What is the easiest and most convenient way to own these companies? In my opinion, investors should buy shares in mutual funds and variable annuities that own these great businesses. That way you won't have to worry about when to buy or sell or what company to pick. The mutual fund manager will do all that for you. All you have to do is sit back and collect those dividend checks when you need them.

How do you know which mutual fund to buy shares in? That's the job of your financial advisor. Because there are more than 8,000 mutual funds to pick from, it has become very complicated. Many mutual funds pay little or no dividend at all, and most have no long-term proven track record. You shouldn't go out and blindly buy a stock mutual fund thinking it owns the companies that pay rising dividends. Most do not.

If you are a long-term investor who plans on living a long time in retirement, dividends might just be the answer to your rising income needs. None of us knows for sure how long we are going to live. So if we do live a long time in retirement, dividends should help keep our standard of living rising throughout the rest of our lives.

Rising Income for Life

One of the key financial goals of IFLs (Investor-for-Life) is that they want and need rising income for the rest of their lives. In addition to receiving the rising dividends that many companies pay, investors don't have to, and normally shouldn't, buy only dividend paying stocks.

If one is to be diversified among the best small, large and international companies in the world, it is going to be nearly impossible to achieve rising income from all these companies from dividends alone. Why? Many small, large and international companies pay very small dividends or pay none at all. Consequently, one cannot adequately diversify and rely on dividends alone to achieve rising income.

Rx for Risk: Rising Income

A rising income strategy called *systematic withdrawal* is an excellent investment strategy for IFLs who want rising income and still want to be diversified among the best companies in the world. Let's run through a hypothetical example. We will make an assumption that the stock market will grow at 10% per year.

$100,000 is invested initially into stock mutual funds and the investor will start out by taking 6% of the value of the account.

	Year 1	Year 2	Year 3	Year 4	Year 5
Principal	$100,000	$104,000	$108,160	$112,486	$116,984
Rate of return	10%	10%	10%	10%	10%
Gain	$10,000	$10,400	$10,816	$11,248	$11,698
Income taken out	-6,000	-6,240	-6,490	-6,750	-7,020
Gain left over to reinvest	$4,000	$4,160	$4,326	$4,498	$4,678

In addition to receiving $6,000 the first year, the IFL received rising income the following years because the account principal grew due to the gain left over each year. This gain was reinvested to make the principal grow.

This is how the IFL achieves rising income and still gets his or her principal to grow over the long-term. You can see that the investor's income started at $6,000 the first year and gradually increased to $7,020 in the fifth year! Imagine what it could grow to over a 20-year period. That type of income is just what the advisor ordered to combat the inevitable rising cost of living.

Obviously, companies' stock prices do not go up at a nice consistent 10% per year. About one out of every three and a half years there will be a temporary decline in the market (to shake out the non-believers). Also, some of the increases will be larger than 10%. These fluctuating, yearly returns will change the income and principal balances.

Investors should ask their financial advisor for results from good (1991-1995) and bad (1970-1974) times to see exactly how those numbers can change. Obviously, the longer your time frame, the more consistent your results should be. IFLs who are in their early 60s have a life expectancy of 20 more years, and thus will likely have plenty of time to let the markets run their course and allow the great companies in the world to reward them with rising income and principal growth.

Insurance for the IFL with Rising Income

One of the legitimate negatives for the rising income strategy is the potential of selling shares when the stock market declines, as in a bear market. Obviously investors want to prevent selling shares of stocks when they are temporarily down. How can this be done in the rising income strategy?

If an IFL is retired and is in the stage of taking income rather than accumulating shares, a provision to the strategy is needed. A bear market like the one in '73 & '74 lasted for nearly two years. It is important that income-taking IFLs create a money market account that has two years worth of *investment income* in it. That way, when a bear market comes along, the IFL can simply stop selling shares of his stock mutual funds and can begin taking the income from the money market until the bear market has passed.

For example, if an investor had $200,000 to deposit in the rising income strategy, the investor might keep around $12,000 ($200,000 x 6% x 2 yrs) in the money market account. Two or three year's worth of investment income should be enough to ride out a bear market.

 **POP QUIZ** **(Just to see if you are paying attention.)**

Quickly, which of these two investments is *safer*?

1) Stocks that average 10% per year for the rest of your life, or

2) Fixed income investments like CDs and bonds that average 5% per year for the rest of your life.

If you answered (1) you are on your way to becoming an IFL (Investor-for-Life), because 10% per year will provide you with more income and principal growth for the rest of your life than will 5% per year.

Which of the two previous investments is more *risky*?

Right! (2) is the right answer. Fixed income investments have historically earned less than half of what stocks have averaged. Because their returns are significantly less (actually negative after taxes & inflation in many years) and their income is fixed, the risk that your income won't keep up with the rising cost of living is great.

Chapter 8: The Investment TimeFrame

**"When we're young, days seem short and years seem long.
When we're old, days seem long and years seem short."**
- Unknown -

The **INVESTOR-FOR-LIFE (IFL)**

When most people do planning for their investments, one of the issues they need to deal with is their *timeframe* for investing. Most people's definition of a long-term timeframe is usually 'until retirement' or 'for 15 years' or something of that nature. Those examples might be accurate for the investor with a specific goal in mind, but many times the answer becomes confused with the real issue of investment planning, which is life-long planning.

It is important that goal-focused planning fit into one's investment planning. For example, a person may need to buy a new car in the future or want to pay for a college education for a child or grandchild at a certain date. There can be many reasons why there may be a specific goal and date for an investment timeframe that is fixed and will terminate. It is, however, equally important for investors to realize that most of their investments are meant to support themselves and their family for the rest of their lives.

Interestingly, most investors don't realize that they have a good chance of living well into their eighties. Since most people retire around 60 to 65, they will have 20 years or more of living in retirement! The costs of living are going to rise during this time. It will be very important to get your income to rise to pay for the rising costs of living. Since all of us need to deal with rising costs of living for the rest of our lives, how can there be any other timeframe for your income needs than for the *rest of your life?*

It is this paradigm that is greatly misunderstood. So, I am forced to bring the issue to a head and ask bluntly: "*Do you know exactly when your life will end?*" I would suspect that the great majority of us have *no idea* and so we can only respond to the big question with the big answer, "*I have no idea!*"

This should lead us to the inevitable answer to the question of "*What is the time-frame for most of your investments?*"

…And the answer is…

"FOR THE REST OF MY LIFE."

Outside of specific goals, your investments can be structured so they will provide you with a lifestyle of rising income for the *rest of your life.* None of us knows for sure how long we are going to live. We may have a few clues by looking at our genes, but there is not a perfect link to our ancestors' pasts. We can look around and clearly see that people are living longer today. Many of us have parents and grandparents, friends, or other relatives that are living well into their late eighties and nineties. We must plan for life to be potentially very long. We cannot afford to run out of money or income when we are 78 years old and may still be living ten years later, wondering not only where time went but where did all the money go.

Because we cannot predict our deaths with any great certainty, don't we inevitably have to plan to keep some money positioned so it can pay us rising income for the rest of our lives?

As investors, all of us have the potential to become and to stay financially independent. None of us wants to be a burden for our children or grand-children. That is why it is vitally important that we set the time frame for our investment planning for the *rest of our lives*. If we could somehow keep inflation (i.e. food & medical costs, etc.) fixed, rising income wouldn't be such a problem. Unfortunately, the *costs of living* are going to *rise* for the rest of your life and, because of this, most people cannot afford to live on a fixed income.

Take a look at how grocery costs have risen over the years. In 1977 four bags of groceries containing items such as soup, cereal, soap, tissue, soft drinks, coffee, bread etc. cost $13.98. Twenty years later, those exact four bags of groceries cost $64.28. That is an increase (inflation) of about 5.85% per year! How much will those same four bags of groceries cost in another 20 years? Try around $200.00! And four bags of groceries don't go very far. They certainly wouldn't last very long in my household!

If you believe that you will need *rising income* for the *rest of your life* and you agree that you have no idea when your life is going to end, I hereby encourage you to become an official *Investor-for-Life* **(IFL).**

To be an IFL, investors must put faith in the great companies in the U.S. and around the world. It is only these companies' stock prices and dividends that will provide the *rising income & growth* that you will need for the *rest of your life*. If investors average 10% per year return on their investments for the rest of their lives, they should be able to keep their income and principal growing faster than taxes and inflation and thus, keep their standard of living rising. To see exactly how this works, be sure to read the chapter on diversification for the Investor-for-life (IFL).

Many investors (would-be IFLs) are worried about the temporary de-clines of companies' stock prices. Let me ask, "Do you believe that stock prices will go down and stay down forever?" And, "What does the temporary decline of stocks *today* have to do with the *rising in-come* and *principal growth* you will receive during the next five, 10, 20,

30 or 40 years while you are visiting your children, grandchildren, taking vacations and living life?"

For example, when you go to the grocery store, do you go with your portfolio statement showing the current value of the principal or,

*do you go with the **income check** that your portfolio is sending you each month?*

If you live beyond the temporary decline (even if you feel like you won't), it won't matter very much. The market will eventually rise as it always has, and your life and income needs will continue to move on.

How about the other scenario that makes us a little nervous - that our lives will end at the moment stock prices have temporarily declined? For the deceased, it won't matter. The money simply gets passed on to his or her heirs or beneficiaries (you can't take it with you, you know).

Many times, the beneficiary is the spouse. For the spouse who is still living, the *temporary decline* is nothing more than *temporary*. The surviving spouse is now the person who will *need rising income* for the rest of his or her life. So again, life and the market just continue.

If the investments are to be passed on to beneficiaries or heirs other than the spouse, one can structure the bequeaths so the inheritors of the investments can keep the rising income and growth investments for their future as well. In the event of inheriting the assets when the market is down, they can simply hold on and wait for the market to inevitably in-crease.

Because your costs of living will rise for the *rest of your life*, your income must rise as well. For the average 60-year old, that means 20 or more years of rising income. The average 50-year old is staring at 30+ years of rising income needs.

Do you see the value of the new paradigm? Outside of specific short-term investment goals, there can be only *one* investment time-frame for investors and their investment planning and that is for the **rest of your life.**

Chapter 9: Diversification for the IFL (Investor-for-Life)

Behold the fool said, 'Put not all your eggs in one basket' – which is a manner of saying, 'Scatter your money and your attention;' but the wise man said, 'Put all your eggs in one basket' and

-'WATCH THAT BASKET.'-
Mark Twain

As the Investor For Life (IFL) knows, he or she wants and needs income to rise throughout his or her life. Since we don't know how long we are going to live, the IFL realizes that his or her investments are most likely going to need to provide a rising income for a long, long time.

The IFL has faith in the great companies in the US and around the world. Because of the great rising income these companies can pay, IFLs realize that a significant portion of their money needs to be deposited into the shares of these great companies. The big question for most people is how to diversify among these companies.

The answer is simple but not obvious. Many people get advice that sounds something like this: put some of your money in growth, some in growth & income and some in aggressive, etc. While I don't disagree with the basic concept, I think investors can increase their potential for growth and rising income by diversifying more astutely and systematically.

To start out, there are five basic areas of the stock market:

Large Company Growth   **Large Company Value**
Small Company Growth   **Small Company Value**

International

I realize there are many other classes that could be fit in such as mid-company growth and value and emerging markets, but in terms of taking advantage of the market's permanent ups and temporary downs and keeping a portfolio simple and efficient, these five categories will work perfectly.

How is each of the five categories different?

The **large company growth** manager is looking for large companies like Disney and Microsoft whose earnings will grow no matter what the economy is doing. They are not interested in steel and automobiles whose industries are largely at the mercy of the economic cycle. They invest in the large growth bullies that will dominate in any market.

The **large company value** manager is looking for steel, mortar, plant and equipment. The idea of investing in a sneezing, wheezing, wet behind-the-ear allergy researcher at Pfizer isn't their idea of a good time. Value companies earnings cycle along with changes in economic activity to a great degree. They like companies like Ford and John Deere.

The **small company growth** manager isn't interested in today's Microsoft or McDonald's. He is interested in tomorrow's little Intel which is run by entrepreneurs who don't understand the word *can't*. He would rather buy 50 small companies for the price of one big one.

The **small company value** manager isn't interested in paying a gazillion times earnings for a small technowizz company whose ideas are barely in the testing stage. He would rather buy the under-researched, misunderstood companies that are ready for big profits. He would rather buy the small companies that outsource to John Deere and Ford.

Diversification for the IFL (Investor-for-Life)

The **International** manager could care less about the good old US of A. The thought of buying stocks in an economy that is growing at about $2^1/2\%$ per year is absurd! He would rather buy companies in the Far East like China which is growing three times as fast! Most of the world's largest banks trade overseas. Many of the world's largest chemical companies are headquartered outside the U.S. He would rather buy companies which will be profiting from the breakdown of the Berlin wall, not the breakdown of talks between the Democrats and Republicans.

So which area is best? **All of them. It depends.** Remember, *all markets move in cycles.* The point of the chart below is to show the cyclicality of stock returns over a given timeframe. There is not normally a perfect relationship over five year periods. Big, small and international companies stock prices always cycle, but their periods of under-and-out performance is hard to predict over short periods of time like a year or two. Within the basic areas of stocks, there will always be one area that is **outperforming** the others. And, there will always be one area that is **underperforming** the other areas.

Take a look at this insightful chart:

Objective	1986 – 1990	1991 – 1995
International	23.2%	10.3%
Large Company	10.7%	15.9%
Small Company	4.7%	20.4%

If it were 1990, in which area would you most likely have been interested in adding money? If you could have chosen between an investment that went up 23.2% or 4.7% per year for the last five years, which area would you have been more easily convinced to buy?

I'm compelled to ask you a very important question: do you want to buy the area that has gone up the *most* over the *last* block of time? Or, would you rather add money to the area that will likely go up the *most* over the *next* block of time. This is the hardest issue for investors to get used to. Successful, astute investors actually need to buy things that are currently under-performing.

Interestingly, the paradigm of wanting to buy the investment that has just gone up the most is shared by a majority of people. I'm sure you can guess which of the areas received the most **inflow** of money in the years of 1989-1990. You guessed it – international mutual funds had the largest inflow of money in 1989-1990. The astute IFLs did just the opposite and bought under-performance in 1989-1990. They added money to the area of small company.

Remember that one area is not better than another. Small companies are not better or worse than large companies. They are all just different and their stock prices rise and fall at different times in the economic cycle. *They are all great investments, just at different times.*

Buy Underperformance?

One of the big mistakes that investors and advisors make is recommending the *best* mutual fund. First, in terms of being the best (the fund that has gone up the most over the *last* block of time), there can be only *one* fund that is truly the best over the last block of time. What is the last block of time? Generally, most people will typically use the last one, three or five-year performance figures. What are they really telling you? What **not to buy.** Since it has been an out-performer for the last block of time, it will most likely be an under-performer for the next block of time. That is why you rarely see or hear the same 'best' fund mentioned year-after-year.

Do you really want to buy the fund or funds in a certain category that has **gone up the most** during the **last block of time**? Let's mull this one over because it doesn't get much more important than this.

Or, would you rather buy the fund in the category that is going to **go up the most** over the **next block of time?**

Let me give you a quick test to see if this all makes sense. If I gave you a call one evening and you were at home watching Seinfeld and I asked, "Do you have a minute for the phone?" and you said, "Sure!" and I said, "I have a mutual fund that went down 9% two years ago and went up only 1% last year. I think you should buy some". You would say, "Have you lost your marbles!" and would most likely, and unpolitely I might add, hang up and go back to the much more interesting Kramer. But…

If I gave you that same call and mentioned that I had a fund that went up 30% two years ago and 25% last year, would you be more likely to listen and say "That's interesting. Tell me more, or let's get together for a cup of coffee to talk about this investment."

The following is the performance figures for a popular mutual fund. Which year would you invest in this fund?

1986	1987	1988	1989	1990	1991
+18.5	+4.8	+16.1	+29.1	-9.8	+40.8

Keep in mind, I'm not suggesting that you invest your money in mutual funds that are under-performers relative to other funds in the same category. *I think it is very important that your mutual fund performs at least average or better relative to funds in a similar category.* If you aren't sure about your own particular fund, then you should have a financial advisor do an analysis to see how it measures up to others. What is most important, however, is that you add money to the fund in the area that is currently under-performing.

How About the Indexes?

Stock index funds are mutual funds that are made up of a basket of stocks that represent a certain index. These index funds are *unmanaged*. Unmanaged means that there isn't a money manager making buy-and-sell decisions on behalf of the shareholders of the mutual fund.

An issue often brought up by some advisors is that of putting your money in a mutual fund like a large company index fund. While this is a fine strategy for someone who is able to invest in only one fund, it surely doesn't enable you to invest in all five basic areas of the market. The large company index funds are generally made up of *large company* growth and value stocks. If you want to add money to the area that is under-performing, how are you going to do it when you have an index fund that captures only one or two of the stock categories? You can't.

This philosophy would also apply to the application of index-type funds that are considered the total market index funds. Total market index funds invest in small and large company stocks in the U.S. These types of funds are also *unmanaged*.

While it is true that a portion of this type of fund is invested in some of the five basic stock categories, *how can one take advantage of the area that is under-performing?* If you added money to this type of fund, you would be adding to *all the areas*, the areas that are up as well as down. Only a small portion of your contribution would be going to the under-performing area and *most would be going to the out-performing areas*.

Adding money to the area that is out-performing today is not what you want. You would want all of the additions to the account going to the under-performing area. That is why I don't believe an investor can simply just put his or her money in one or two funds and be truly diversified and be able to do what the most successful investors do: out-perform in the *next block of time.* The IFL needs four or five stock mutual funds to diversify effectively.

Where the Rubber Meets the Road

The concept of trying to reduce fluctuation is a strange concept to all great IFLs. The obsession of experts recommending that investors reduce fluctuation risk flies *right in the face* of achieving great investment success. For the IFL, fluctuation of a portfolio represents *opportunity*, not loss. Astute investors realize that *fluctuation is not loss* (unless you panic and sell) and is in fact the great opportunity to buy stocks in the area of the portfolio that is temporarily down. In fact, the more fluctuation an IFL can get, the more opportunities he or she has to take advantage of those temporary declines; and **the deeper the decline, the better the future return.**

If your main goal is to try to reduce fluctuation because you are worried about losing money, you would be better off diversifying like the traditional investor. History, repeatedly, has shown that stock market declines *are frequent* and always temporary, **never permanent**. In 1933, the Dow Jones Industrial Average hit 40; by 1998 the Dow crossed 9,000. I couldn't count the number of times it *went down*, but it never *stayed down*. And that, in the end, is all that matters. With confidence and reasoning, we can also say that the Dow will hit 50,000. Exactly at what date no one knows, *but we know it is inevitable.*

By the way, with the Dow Jones at 9,000, it would take about 20 years (2018) to reach 50,000 if the market increases at a rate of 9% per year!

In keeping with the philosophy of the IFL paradigm, the idea of buying bonds (especially when interest rates are low) to reduce fluctuation is odd. And, unfortunately, when stock prices are declining, interest rates are usually rising; consequently, *both stocks and bond prices are declining in tandem.* It's just that bond prices generally decline a little less. So if an investor had 50% of his or her portfolio in stocks and 50% in bonds in 1974, per Ibbotson, the following resulted:

50% stocks / 50% bonds = **- 14.8%**

100% stocks = **- 26.5%**

At some point in the future this scenario could happen again. Whether your portfolio is down 15% or 26% doesn't really matter too much (unless you needed all of your money on the exact day these declines were at their lowest point). In either case, whether the investor is down 15% or 26% is basically a non-issue for short-term oriented investors who don't understand that market declines are temporary. They aren't sleeping at night in either scenario (they are up watching infomercial re-runs).

If you have faith in the great companies in the U.S. and around the world and believe that market declines are temporary, you won't make the *Big Mistake* (selling at the low) in either scenario and bail out. The IFL is not affected by the decline. The difference between -15% and -26% is relevant only in respect to the increased opportunity that -26% presents.

Over the past 50 years ending 1997, per Ibbotson, here's a look at the annual returns for the major asset classes:

Small stocks	=	+ 12.4%
Large stocks	=	+ 10.3%
Bonds	=	+ 5.7%
CDs	=	+ 5.0%
Savings	=	+ 3.0%

The concept of returns for a portfolio is quite simple. You don't need all those fancy shmancy asset allocation/diversification/portfolio ratios to fig-ure out how to obtain good long-term returns. Simply,

The more money you have in stocks, the higher your overall return in the long-term.

If you add bonds and other fixed-income assets, you will reduce some temporary declines, but at the high cost of the great permanent ups! For the great accumulators of wealth, *the greater the temporary decline, the greater the opportunity for your portfolio to out-perform in the next block of time.*

How to Diversify

Going back to our original five basic areas of stocks, I think you have a good idea of an optimum strategy to diversify. The IFL's portfolio would have money in each of the following areas:

Large Company Growth	**Large Company Value**
Small Company Growth	**Small Company Value**

International

The strategy is to develop a portfolio that includes a portion of your money in each of the five basic areas. That way, your portfolio will always have an area that is currently out-performing the other areas. At the same time, *your portfolio will always have an area that is under-performing; that is how you know you are truly diversified.* Your strategy, of course, would be to add to the area that is currently *under-performing.*

Diversification for the Retired IFL

For those of you who are retired IFLs and are worried that you cannot add money, or will need money when the market is declining, you will need to alter your strategy slightly. Since you are getting rising income for your living expenses, you wouldn't want to compound your portfolio's temporary declines by selling shares in a sharp decline.

As I mentioned in the Rx for Risk chapter, retired IFLs should keep at least two years worth of *investment income* in their money market account. That way, if the market runs up against the grizzly of all bear markets, like the one in 1973-74 where the market declined 40% over two years, you could just stop taking income from the stock shares and start taking income out of the money market until the market finally resumes its permanent upward march. Two-to-three years of investment income should be more than enough for you to weather a bear market.

The average bear market decline normally lasts about eight months. So having the flexibility of two-to-three years worth of investment income should be more than adequate. This money market balance is the insurance that allows you to be an IFL and still take advantage of the great long-term returns of stocks while not having to worry about the temporary bear market.

Chapter 10: Don't Fear the Bear

October. This is one of the peculiarly dangerous months to speculate in stocks. The others are July, January, September, April, November, May, March, June, December, August, and February.
Mark Twain

October. This is the one of the peculiarly best months to buy stocks. The others are July, January, September, April, November, May, March, June, December, August, and February.
Dan Geffre

What do Real Bear Markets Look Like?

A sharp stock market decline is normally triggered by a totally unexpected event. In the past these events have materialized from events such as the foreign market crises, presidents being shot, interest rates unexpectedly rising etc.

Unless stock valuations are high, which is normally the case in sharp declines, negative news doesn't push stocks down very much. It is the period in which stock prices are high relative to earnings that the potential for an unexpected event causes these temporary sharp declines.

Based on the recent experience of the 1990's, many investors consider a 10% drop that lasts a month or two something of a bear market. This is not the case when we look back at the bear markets of the last 50 years. Since the end of World War II, *there have been 10% price declines on average every other year. This would suggest that declines of this magnitude should be considered a normal event.*

A more realistic definition of a bear market is a temporary decline of 15% or more. There have been 14 of these declines since 1950. That translates to a 15% decline about every 3½ years. Again, long-term investors should consider these temporary declines ordinary and consistent.

So how long did these temporary buying opportunities last? The longest lasted 21 months (1973-74) and the shortest was two months (1987). However, the average decline lasted eight months. This means that IFLs have, on average, eight great months to buy shares of stocks at very *attractive prices.*

How far did the average bear market decline? The biggest decline was 48% (1973-74). Of course, by definition the smallest decline was 15% (1953 & 1975). The average decline was 24%. Obviously, these are significant opportunities to buy shares. They should always be taken advantage of, and IFLs who are adding money to their retirement plans and stock mutual funds on a monthly basis are doing just that.

Of great importance and significance is the relatively short time-span that the market took to recoup most of the declines. *On average it took 13 months to recover 100% of the decline.* In other words, if you decided to go to the North Pole for a one-year vacation and checked your stock portfolio before you left and then took a look once you returned home, you wouldn't have even noticed that anything happened. Thirteen months is an extremely brief period for the IFL and, consequently, these declines offer nothing less than a great opportunity to buy shares of great companies at more reasonable prices. For the IFL who isn't accumulating shares, it is a great opportunity to *do nothing*.

So what happens after one of these bear markets? The market eventually goes on to new record highs *every time*. As mentioned previously, these bear markets are unexpected, so investors cannot predict when they are going to happen. Should one just wait for a bear market to happen before investing?

NO! More money has been lost by being out of the stock market during its great advances than by being in the market during its temporary declines. Unfortunately, even those so-called experts who make a living trying to predict stock market movements are rarely accurate (if they are, it's pure luck). Because market declines are always temporary and unexpected, the IFL knows that market timing is futile.

 ## COME ON BEAR MARKET!

For the great accumulators of wealth, I cannot think of a better scenario than for stock prices to decline for about eight months or so, can you? Sorry, but the only other scenario is the **fairy tale** where the stock market rises each and every year in marching band form at 12% for the rest of your life.

Why should the faithful accumulators of wealth adding money to their retirement plans and mutual funds not worry every month when their brokerage statement arrives showing its value has declined again? Let me ask you an important question. Would you rather pay *more* or *less* for each share of stock or mutual fund that you purchase each month? In other words, if you were adding $100 per month, would you rather pay $10 or $8 for each share?

Let's take a look at how dollar-cost-averaging works in relation to price fluctuation. Again, if we know that the stock market is going to increase over the long-term (for the rest of our lives), wouldn't we want temporary, short-term sharp declines? Here's how these declines work toward our advantage.

Month	Amount Invested	Share Price	Shares Purchased
January	$100	$10	10
February	$100	$ 8	12.5
March	$100	$ 6	16.6
April	$100	$ 6	16.6
May	$100	$ 9	11.1
June	$100	$10	10
Six-month total	**$600**	**$10**	**76.8**

Let's do an analysis now that the share price is back to $10 per share. You've invested a total of $600 and the total value of your portfolio six months later is worth $768 (76.8 shares x $10 p/share). As is obvious, had these declines been even *greater* from February through May, your profits would have been even *higher* because your share prices would have been lower, and, consequently, you would have purchased more shares in the decline! For the great accumulators of wealth (those adding money on a regular basis) **the greater the temporary decline, the better the future return!**

As the IFL knows, the value of these companies' stock prices is going to be significantly higher in the long-term (i.e. $10 p/share will eventually be worth $67 p/share if the market increases at 10% per year for the next 20 years). Hence, accumulators of wealth, those that are adding money to their mutual funds and retirement accounts, are enjoying temporary stock market declines.

If you remember that stock market declines are always temporary (it's the increases that are permanent) and that the declines represent buying opportunities, you can enhance your portfolio's future return by taking advantage of these declines. This leads me to a *simple*, yet *profound* equation:

More declines = More profits
&
Bigger declines = Bigger profits

If I still haven't convinced you that temporary declines are a reason to be happy, I have some good news for the bears of the world. While short-term declines can add significant profits, it is important to recognize that it is *never a bad time to make a good investment*. I would like to introduce you to **'Louie the Loser'** who is brought to us by a study done by the American Funds Group.

Louie the Loser was the most unlucky person alive. He cancelled his dental insurance right before his tooth flared up. He misses planes but catches colds. When it comes to investing, Louie the Loser never times anything right.

Every year for the past 20 years, he's invested $10,000 in his growth & income mutual fund on the worst possible day to invest – the day the stock market peaked. But why is Louie smiling anyway? Because his investment has done very well – nearly as well, in fact, as it would have if he had picked the best days to invest. Take a look: ☞ ☞ ☞

(Don't Forget to Come Back!)

I think I can safely say that none of us would manage to be as unlucky as Louie. It is more likely that our monthly or annual contributions would be somewhere in between – some at the top, some at the bottom and a lot in the middle. However, it is important to point out that Louie is smiling 20 years later because he discovered that *time in the market, not timing, is what matters*.

As you can see, there isn't a bad time to make a good investment for long-term traditional investors and IFLs. To accumulate and preserve wealth, investors should add money as it becomes available. Fortunately, when a temporary decline does come along, it is a rare opportunity to increase your portfolio's future return.

Worst-Day Investments (market highs)

Date of Market high	Cumulative Investment	Account Value on 12/31
9/8/78	10,000	8,323
10/5/79	20,000	19,212
11/20/80	30,000	32,496
4/27/81	40,000	41,689
12/27/82	50,000	65,247
11/29/83	60,000	87,809
1/6/84	70,000	103,628
12/16/85	80,000	147,920
12/2/86	90,000	189,462
8/25/87	100,000	207,428
10/21/88	110,000	244,658
10/9/89	120,000	326,136
7/16/90	130,000	337,556
12/31/91	140,000	436,902
6/1/92	150,000	477,729
12/29/93	160,000	542,994
1/31/94	170,000	553,346
12/13/95	180,000	732,608
12/27/96	190,000	884,008
8/6/97	200,000	1,157,701

Average Annual return: + 15.7%

Best-Day Investments (market lows)

Date of Market low	Cumulative Investment	Account Value on 12/31
2/28/78	10,000	11,581
11/7/79	20,000	24,334
4/21/80	30,000	42,319
9/25/81	40,000	52,875
8/12/82	50,000	84,163
1/3/83	60,000	112,808
7/24/84	70,000	131,731
1/4/85	80,000	188,851
1/22/86	90,000	241,874
10/19/87	100,000	265,326
1/20/88	110,000	312,000
1/3/89	120,000	416,422
10/11/90	130,000	430,103
1/9/91	140,000	557,150
10/9/92	150,000	606,470
1/20/93	160,000	687,842
4/4/94	170,000	699,261
1/30/95	180,000	926,089
1/10/96	190,000	1,117,238
4/11/97	200,000	1,463,113

Average Annual Return: + 17.2%

Chapter 11: Ignoring Chicken Little

 **'The sky is falling! The sky is falling!'** Chicken Little's cry seems to race through the world's stock markets every year. The pessimists are always looking for a reason not to invest in the greatest companies in the world.

In the last 55 years the U.S. stock market (big company stocks), per Ibbotson Associates, averaged over 13% per year. The following major events were *unjustified* reasons to stay out of the stock market over the years.

- Pearl Harbor was bombed in December 1941.
- The Russians launched Sputnik in October 1957. That vaulted them into space ahead of the U.S.
- The Berlin Wall was erected in August 1961.
- President Kennedy was assassinated in November 1963.
- President Nixon resigned after the Watergate scandal in August 1974.
- The nuclear disaster struck at Three Mile Island in March 1979.
- The Dow Jones Industrial Average dropped a record 508 points (22%) in October 1987.

Obviously the previous events were significant, but the ramifications on the stock markets' returns were temporary. Moreover, the stock market did very well through these crises.

To show you how *little Chicken Little's cries really mean*, take a look

95

at one of the great bull markets (over 17% per year) the country has ever seen, and observe some of the short-term reasons why many didn't want to invest in any given year. As you can see, not much has happened in terms of crises compared to the last six decades.

1984 – The Dow Jones Industrial Average is over 1250. It's an all-time high and I missed it!

1985 – There haven't been this many bank failures since the 1930's.

1986 – The Federal Deficit is over 200 Billion.

1987 – A Dow at 2000 is ridiculous. I'm not getting in!

1988 – Where were you during the crash? I was out of the market.

1989 – There's talk of bailing out the S &L's. I'm bailing out.

1990 – The '80s are over, but the junk bond problems aren't.

1991 – We're days away from war with Iraq. Could there be a worse time to invest?

1992 – Invest in stocks? Maybe you haven't heard, we're in a recession.

1993 – We are swearing in a new President and a new party. I'm swearing off the stock market.

1994 – Let government run health care? American business will never recover.

1995 – Inflation and interest rates are going up, up, up. Stocks are at an all-time high! The weak dollar and derivative shake out.

1996 – Are you kidding, stocks are at an all-time high! We're getting ready for the big crash.

1997 – There's no way stocks can go higher this year. Stocks are at an all-time high!

1998 – The Asian economic and currency crisis will ruin us all. Stocks can't keep going up.

Allowing your emotions to determine your investment decisions because of short-term unexpected events is a very *big mistake*. There will always be reasons people can use to justify staying out of the market. Many of those events had, at the most, a short-term effect.

For the rest of your life, you will hear Chicken Little proclaiming the sky is falling again and again. These cries will come in many different forms as they have in the last 15 years. The most pessimistic will be proclaiming that the end is near and the *death of stocks* is about to commence. Ignore the *sky is falling* journalism. They're just selling newspaper, magazines, and headlines.

Can the Sky Fall ?

A big fear many people have is: Can I lose *all my money* (in the stock market)?

Yes…. If you do something foolish like put *all* your money in the latest hot stock or investment tip that you overheard being talked about at the water cooler yesterday.

Absolutely NOT… If you put your money in a diversified portfolio of common stocks from the greatest companies in the U.S. and around the world.

What would be the chances of 1,000 of the world's leading companies (Coca-Cola, 3M, GE, Microsoft, Proctor & Gamble etc.) going bankrupt *all at once* within the next year (*or your lifetime for that matter*)? If you had your money diversified in five mutual funds that each owned around 200 of the world's greatest companies in their category (Large Co. Growth/Value, Small Co. Growth/Value, International), the chances would be…

One in a gazillion

And if you think there is a good chance, you might as well stop reading here. By the way, if all 1,000 of the world's strongest companies went bankrupt at once, I think we could safely say that the thousands of smaller companies would be in trouble as well.

Is this anything like your day?

When I got up this morning, I turned off the electric alarm clock **(General Electric)**, showered, shaved **(Gillette)** and brushed my teeth **(Colgate)**. I whipped up a batch of eggs, Jimmy Dean sausage **(Sara Lee)** and a cup of Maxwell House coffee **(Phillip Morris)** and drove to work in my **(Ford)** Taurus.

On the way to work, the cellular phone rang **(Motorola)**. It was my spouse reminding me that because the other car was in the shop getting a new starter **(Genuine Parts Co.)**, I needed to stop by the store **(Wal-Mart)** to pick up a Little Tykes slide **(Rubbermaid)** for our son's birthday. We also needed Coppertone **(Schering Plough)** for our vacation next week.

When I got to the office, I turned on my computer **(Compaq)** and returned a few calls **(baby bell telephone companies)** on my telephone **(AT&T)**. Before I knew it, my watch **(Dayton's Dept. Store)** showed that it was time for lunch. I stopped by the ATM machine **(Norwest Banks)** before meeting a friend for a quick hamburger and a soft drink **(McDonald's & Coca-Cola)**. On the way home from work, I stopped at the gas station **(Mobil)** to fill my car.

At home that night, I cooked supper while my spouse did a load of laundry **(Whirlpool)**. Later, we munched on Pringles **(Proctor & Gamble)** and drank Mountain Dew **(PepsiCo)** in front of the **(Sony)** television I bought at the store **(JC Penney)**.

Take a look at your day. Which companies do you support? The only way for *all* of these companies to go bankrupt is if everyone quit using their products *entirely* – which means we all have to quit living life *at once*. As long as we keep living life and using products we need, there will always be companies competing and making a profit from those items. *We use a lot of products every day!*

Again, what are the chances that stock prices are going to go down and *stay down*? It's counterintuitive to think that you can lose all your money when you are diversified among all the great companies in the world. As a whole, their declines can only be temporary. **Ignore Chicken Little!**

Chapter 12: Life Insurance

Life insurance is a topic many investors don't particularly like to deal with. It is, however, a very important part of life-long financial planning. In addition to protecting your family while they are most dependent on your well-being, life insurance can be used very effectively in estate planning. It is not the scope of this chapter to discuss its intricacies. Suffice it to say, however, that life insurance planning should be taken very seriously and incorporated into your life-long financial planning.

Term Life Insurance

Term life insurance is a contract between an investor and an insurance company to protect survivors against hardship due to the death of the insured. The insurance proceeds are paid to the beneficiary, or beneficiaries, free of ordinary income tax, at the time of death. There are no investment attributes to term life insurance and no cash build up, which makes the initial premium less expensive than that of permanent insurance. Term life insurance is often referred to as temporary life insurance.

Health and age determine the amount of premiums payable under a term insurance plan. The premiums will increase with advancing age. The insurance company generally cannot cancel the policy, but the policy owner may cancel at any time. The insured must meet the company's insurability standards at the time of purchase.

Term insurance is primarily suited for investors with short-term life insurance needs (ten years or less) or those with a long-term need but whose budget won't allow for the higher premiums that permanent insurance commands. Ideally, the term insurance buyer will eventually become self-insured.

One of the main features of term insurance is its low cost. Term insurance is inexpensive. This is especially attractive to younger investors who have a smaller net worth or annual income. Term life insurance may also be convertible to a permanent policy without insurability. This is advantageous because an investor could start out with a term policy and, as time goes on, choose to convert to a permanent policy when his or her income is high enough to afford the permanent policy for his or her long-term insurance needs.

Permanent Life Insurance

In contrast to term life insurance, *permanent life insurance* provides insurance protection over one's entire lifetime. Interestingly, permanent life insurance is term insurance with a savings component added to it called cash value. Investors pay the term insurance cost with each premium payment. But because investors are over-paying in the beginning so they can keep their premium payments even in the future, the extra money above the term insurance cost is placed into the cash value account to earn interest. Essentially, you are over-paying now so you don't have to increase payments in the future.

Permanent life insurance is available in two basic forms: universal life and whole life. A hybrid of universal life is called variable life (the cash value is invested in mutual funds) and is becoming more and more popular. Although both forms offer protection over the lifetime of the insured, their structures are different. Generally speaking, universal life will permit a lower cost per thousand of insurance, but its projections are more volatile, which passes on more pricing risk than whole life. Each form has advantages over the other and the selection should be based on the long-term objectives of the insured.

The cash value of permanent life insurance grows tax-deferred. Withdrawals and loans against the value of your policy are, with certain restrictions, free from current taxation. The death benefits pass to the beneficiary free of federal income taxes.

Buying Term Vs Permanent Insurance

There has been a lot of discussion about buying term insurance and investing the difference compared to buying universal life. The concept of buying term and investing the difference is a very interesting idea. Many agents recommend that everyone should only buy term insurance. Others almost exclusively recommend a type of permanent insurance.

I do not believe there is an absolute answer as to which is better. Each situation requires a different strategy. As a general rule, the 'buy term and invest the difference' philosophy works best if the insurance need is short-term. If the insurance need is longer, the permanent insurance can be a better alternative.

The scope of this chapter is not to define which type of insurance, in any given situation, is most appropriate. That is the job of your financial advisor. It is important that investors, when making life-long financial planning decisions, closely examine a number of strategies and determine with their advisor which strategy is most appropriate.

To help with some rules of thumb, investors can start with the following guidelines:

Time-Frame of Insurance Need	Appropriate Insurance
0 – 10 years	Term Life Insurance
10 – 15 years	Term & Permanent Combination
15 + years	Permanent Life Insurance

One last note: If you do have life insurance in force, be sure to review your insurance objectives periodically. It makes sense to have your insurance policies reviewed and analyzed to determine if they are meeting your cost and cash value projections. Your financial advisor can help you do an *in-force illustration*. This analysis will give you important information on how well the insurance policy is performing.

Chapter 13: Estate Planning

Planning for the inevitable distribution of your assets at death is the process known as *estate planning*. It must first be said that the *only time for you to plan for your estate's succession is when you are alive*, because once you are dead, there is no more time to plan. In the event of no planning, the state legislature through the intestacy statutes, will make the decisions for you. The ideal time to do your estate planning is when both spouses are alive, so appropriate provisions can be made with detailed planning.

Unfortunately, many people put off estate planning for two reasons: because they feel they are young and have plenty of time to do it before getting closer to retirement, and because we all think that nothing will happen to us while we are young so we can afford to wait until later. This line of thinking can be very dangerous. It is the unexpected accident (yes I know, obviously, accidents are unexpected, but it seemed to work the best) that catches us by surprise and, in the event of death, it will be too late to do some important planning. The estate planning process should begin when assets begin to accumulate and/or when family members have a responsibility to each other.

Developing Your Estate Plan

To begin, you will need to ask yourself some important questions. Formulating your estate plan requires the assistance of your financial advisor and an experienced estate-planning attorney, but as a first step, the following should be considered for developing your estate plan.

- Do you have a will? Have you reviewed it lately?
- In the event you become incapacitated, do you have a plan in place to make decisions for you?
- In the event that you and/or your spouse become disabled or incapacitated, do you have a plan in place that will provide for the care of your minor or handicapped children?
- Do you want or need a living will?
- Do you have any special instructions for your burial or funeral? Do you have any special bequests?
- Have you reviewed the beneficiaries on your life insurance or retirement plans (especially the contingent beneficiaries)?
- Will the value of your estate be affected by the federal estate tax?
- Is your estate sufficiently liquid to pay estate taxes and/or preserve your family business?

These are the kinds of issues that you will need to deal with to put your *house in order* to protect you and your family at your death. Only through careful planning can you be sure that you and your heirs will be cared for according to your wishes.

An estate plan can help you preserve your estate and reduce unnecessary estate taxes. The estate tax issue is an important one because a significant portion of an estate can be lost *unnecessarily* due to a lack of estate planning. Estate planning can help you avoid probate and allow you to protect your privacy regarding the distribution of your assets. Your estate plan can provide for the management of your estate in the event of disability. It can also help you control the distribution of assets to your heirs and increase the liquidity (insurance planning) of your estate.

What Happens to an Estate Upon Death?

Your estate goes through the process known as probate. Probate is a formal, court-supervised process that distributes assets to your heirs. A will goes through probate to be validated and to allow time for creditors and/or heirs to make claims against the estate. Probate process can last from nine months to two years. It is a public proceeding, meaning the estate's contents are made public.

How does the probate process work? The executor of the estate files a petition. A death notice is then published. A hearing is then held to validate the will. The assets are frozen for inventory. At that time, the assets become inaccessible to the heirs. Real estate owned in another state is probated in the state where the land is owned. The executor then pays all debts, taxes and fees, and files the appropriate tax returns for the estate. Finally, the assets are distributed and the estate is then officially closed.

What happens if I die without a will?

The term that refers to an estate without a will is termed *intestate*. When a person dies intestate, the estate is probated and the state statutes decide where the assets are to be distributed.

What are estate and inheritance taxes?

The *Federal Estate Tax* is a tax owed to the Government for estates over certain levels. Prior to the Tax Payer Relief Act of 1997, every taxpayer was allowed to transfer up to $600,000 in assets free of federal gift and estate taxes. The transfer can be made as a gift during one's lifetime, or at death. In 1998, the estate tax began at $625,000 and incrementally increases until the year 2006 when its level will reach $1,000,000 per person. This tax is payable within nine months of death. Tax rates *start* at 37 percent and increase to 55 percent at the maximum level.

The *State Inheritance Tax* is a tax that is levied by your resident state. The estate pays it before any assets can be distributed.

The *Unified Tax Credit* allows every individual a unified tax credit of $202,050 in 1998 and rising incrementally to the year 2006. This credit means that any estate valued at $625,000 in 1998 (rising incrementally until 2006) or less can be passed to heirs free of federal estate taxes. *This is a "use or lose" credit, which means that if your estate plan didn't make provisions to take advantage of this credit, it can be lost at your death.*

The *Unlimited Marital Deduction* allows an estate to be passed to a surviving spouse without any estate taxes, regardless of the estate's value. This deduction applies only when assets pass directly to the spouse. On the death of the surviving spouse, the entire estate is fully taxable.

Estate-Planning Tools

A **will** is a legal declaration of how a person wishes his or her possessions to be distributed after death. It details exactly how the estate will be distributed. One of the big advantages of a will is that it is inexpensive and relatively easy to draft. Wills allow for special bequests and can provide for the appointment of a guardian for minors or handicapped children. If a designation is not made within the will, the probate court selects a guardian. *That is to say, if a person or family has no will or makes no provision in the will for a guardian for minor children, the court will select a guardian.* If you don't designate a guardian for your minors, you will be leaving all decision-making to the courts that may or may not make the "right" decision in your eyes.

Trusts can be a valuable estate-planning tool that offers an effective way to address the management of assets and issues such as maximizing potential tax savings, planning for incapacity, and probate avoidance. A trust is simply a set of written instructions. There are a number of different types of trusts. The following are just a few common estate-planning trusts:

A *testamentary trust* is a trust established through a will. It only becomes effective upon death.

A *marital deduction trust* is a trust that takes advantage of the deduction that is available for interspousal transfers either during lifetimes or at death. Under federal law, there is complete interspousal exemption for qualifying transfers regardless of the amount.

A *charitable remainder trust* is one of the most commonly used forms of charitable tax planning. The charitable remainder trust offers a way to convert a highly appreciated asset (e.g., real estate or stock) into lifetime income without having to pay capital gains tax on the sale or estate taxes at death. The asset is placed into an *irrevocable trust*, naming one or more charities as beneficiary. The trustee can then sell the assets at full market value without paying taxes and reinvest the proceeds in more income-producing assets. The trust then pays the grantor income from the trust. Upon the grantor's death, the remainder of the trust goes to the designated charity.

An *irrevocable life insurance trust* is established for the purposes of excluding life insurance proceeds from the estate of the insured for estate-tax purposes. It is a type of trust, the corpus of which consists in whole or in part of life insurance policies owned by the trustees and payable to the trust on the death of the insured. The proceeds of the life insurance can then pay taxes that are owed on the estate, etc.

A *revocable living trust* is a document drafted by an attorney that allows any asset placed within it to avoid probate. It is called revocable because the grantor can change it as often as necessary during his or her lifetime. In addition, the grantor can buy, sell, borrow, or transfer assets into or out of the trust as needed. It is a flexible planning tool. One of its biggest advantages is that assets in it avoid probate, thereby keeping its contents and distributions private. Also, it allows the grantor the flexibility of changing it or the assets as he or she wishes. One of the disadvantages is that is has higher initial costs compared to a will and it does take some time and effort to transfer assets into the trust.

One important misconception people have about revocable living trusts is that they reduce estate taxes because they don't go through probate. *This is not true.* **While living trusts do bypass probate, they are part of a decedent's estate and are, therefore, subject to estate taxes.**

Some financial-services firms offer a service called **Transfer-on-Death** (TOD). This beneficiary contract allows *securities and cash in your investment account* to be transferred directly (escaping probate) to named beneficiaries when you die. A TOD account is generally easy to establish. *It avoids the time, expense and publicity of probate.* It doesn't, however, avoid or address estate taxes for large estates. The TOD is less flexible than a trust and cannot handle an entire estate (real estate, personal property etc.). Also, beneficiaries, rather than the estate, are liable for any taxes due resulting from the distribution from the TOD account.

The process of estate planning is a complex one and should be planned with your financial advisor, CPA and estate-planning attorney. It is one of the most important parts of life-long retirement planning.

Chapter 14: Getting Started

Selecting a Financial Advisor

How do you find a financial advisor whose advice you can trust? During the bullish period of the 1980s and '90s, it almost didn't matter whether your financial advisor was a genius, a rocket scientist, or simply somebody's smiling son-in-law. If you had money in the market in the 1980s and '90s, you were almost assured of making money.

With the huge array of new investments available, coupled with the barrage of men and women entering the financial services industry, it is important to find a financial advisor who has the ability to communicate with you and help you understand the complexities of various investment, tax, estate, life insurance and retirement planning issues.

Choosing the right financial advisor is not quite as important as selecting the right spouse… but since the advisor will do much to determine if you are financially comfortable in the future, it is a decision to be taken seriously.

One important attribute your financial advisor should have is *education*. Continuing advanced education will help keep your advisor up-to-date on planning issues and solutions to the financial challenges that lie ahead of you. Designations that certify advanced education are a sign that your advisor is likely serious about his or her profession. One doesn't *need* to have one of these designations, but it might give you an extra comfort level that you need to hire an advisor.

Another possible source for finding a financial advisor may be referrals from your friends or colleagues. It is important, though, for you to do your homework, even with referrals from friends. You need to interview the person they've recommended to get a feel for the way he or she does business.

If you aren't comfortable asking a friend or co-worker for a referral, and haven't come in social contact with a financial advisor, you may need to go out and visit with some of the brokerage firms in your city. You might start by looking in the Yellow Pages under *Stock & Bond Brokers* or *Investment Securities*. Call the offices and ask to speak with one of their financial advisors; then set up an interview appointment. Remember that this is a two-way interview. Not only should the advisor be asking you some questions, but also, importantly, you must interview the advisor to see if you feel comfortable trusting this person with your money.

If you are starting out cold, not knowing a soul, you should interview more than merely one potential advisor... perhaps two or three. This may give you a better perspective on who you think can do the best job of managing your money and advising you with other financial questions.

When you sit down with a prospective advisor, be sure to *ask questions like:*

- How long has he or she been a financial advisor?
- What is his or her education level?
- Does he or she have designations indicating on-going education?
- Where does he or she get information on investments?
- How does he or she keep track and communicate how clients' today are doing?

Importantly, ask the financial advisor what his or her *investment philosophy* is. Is he or she shooting from the hip, or is there a deeper reason for his or her recommendations? Does this philosophy make sense to you?

You should expect the advisor to create and explain an investment plan, or system, that directly meets your needs, not simply pass on the latest hot stock or investment idea. The investment plan should include some type of philosophy on asset allocation and strategy to deal with profits and losses. *The plan should also include fact finding conversations on tax, estate, and insurance planning issues.*

Your advisor should be inquisitive and ask you many in-depth questions. This person is going to need to know a good deal about you. If you're truly serious about getting advice from a financial advisor, it is important that you share not only all of your financial information, but your true feelings toward investing. Without this information, it is impossible to get informed advice from a financial advisor. If he or she doesn't ask much about your financial situation, you would be best off looking around for another perspective.

A qualified financial advisor is going to need to get a look at your total financial picture. He or she would normally ask you to bring in statements of your savings accounts, CDs, and money market accounts. You should also bring in a list of all your assets such as your bonds, stocks and mutual funds so he or she can get a feel for what kind of investing you've previously done.

Once you have described your situation and goals to the financial advisor, listen to his or her reaction and comments. Do they make sense? Can you understand the recommendations or perspectives? Just because you have taken the time to listen to his or her recommendations doesn't mean you have to invest. But if you feel comfortable with his or her philosophy and recommendations, don't procrastinate. Remember, *there is no bad time to make a good investment!*

One way financial advisors get new clients is by cold calling on the telephone. If you have an interest in listening to their ideas over the telephone, go ahead. But you are not obligated to listen. You may choose to end the phone conversation at any time. Never open an account and buy an investment on the phone without ever having met the advisor. You never know, for sure, with whom you are dealing on the other line.

Personally, I think it's worthwhile to meet a financial advisor **face-to-face** before doing business. You are establishing a relationship that will directly affect your future. It might take some effort to arrange the meeting, but after all, it's your financial future we are talking about!

The most important thing you should expect from a financial advisor is *honesty*. It is important that he or she not only communicates to you when the market is up, but also takes the time to explain why your particular investment may be down. You should expect your financial advisor to keep you informed regularly, in good times and bad. *If you feel uncomfortable with the way your account is being handled, it's your responsibility to take the initiative to make a change.*

Your financial advisor should be up-front about how he or she is paid. You can ask how the advisor is compensated. If he or she seems hesitant to offer that information or tries to hide the fees or commissions, you may be dealing with someone who is less than honest, with not necessarily your best interest at heart.

Once you've chosen a financial advisor, it is important that he or she looks at the total picture for you. In addition to the list of savings and investments statements that you've provided him or her, other documents to bring would include *insurance papers*, copy of last year's *tax return*, *will*, and any *trusts* you've set up. These documents will help your advisor make informed financial planning decisions.

A good financial advisor will be worth far more than what you pay in fees. Remember, fees and commissions are how advisors get paid. There is more to investment planning than simply picking a stock or mutual fund. *A good financial advisor will be able to fuse together the many different aspects of life-long financial planning such as tax, estate, insurance and investment planning.*

How Do I Get Started?

As a general rule, regardless of your age, the first thing you need to accomplish is to build up a money market account that will serve as an emergency fund for the future. The amount you keep in this money market depends on your individual needs. Some people need more money available than others do. Keep enough money available to give you peace of mind without sacrificing too much earning a low rate of interest.

If you have children in school, knowing they could need money at any time, it would be wise to keep a larger balance available. Likewise, if you or a dependant are in poor health, a larger emergency fund would be appropriate.

Once you've achieved your desired level of savings in your emergency fund, decide how you are going to invest. If you are starting out with lesser amounts of money, you are probably best off by putting some money systematically in a mutual fund.

Your next decision – which one? If you choose a no-help (no-load) mutual fund, you need to start doing your own research. After deciding on a particular fund that specifically meets your needs relative to fluctuation and return, you must call the mutual fund family to begin the paperwork process. Once you've received the applications, you would need to fill them out and send them your money. They will provide you with confirmations and statements regarding the status of your mutual fund or funds.

If you choose to get advice from a financial advisor, your first job is to find an advisor you're comfortable with. Once you've accomplished that, the financial advisor will take care of setting up the account and guiding you through the investment process. Your financial advisor will be able to give you advice on which investment best fits your needs relative to your total picture.

Once you've accumulated some money in a fund or number of funds, you can choose to diversify by buying individual stocks or bonds. To buy these securities, you must go through a broker/dealer. You can do this two ways: through a *full-service brokerage firm* or a *discount broker*.

If you make all your own decisions, perform your own research and don't want or need any professional advice, then perhaps a discount brokerage may best fit your needs. Discount brokerage firms do not offer many services of full-service brokerages. They may not send you research or suggest a price at which to buy or sell your stock. But generally, they will charge you a lower commission rate than full-service brokerage firms. The commissions usually vary with the size and volume of trading that you do.

If you are fairly new at investing and don't know your way around Wall Street, a traditional full-service brokerage firm is the right choice for you. A financial advisor will advise you on what to buy, what to sell, and when to buy and sell. Many financial advisors can also help you fuse together other aspects of financial planning such as insurance, tax and estate planning.

Chapter 15: Truths of Investing

- **Definition of Risk = Your income *won't rise* as fast as the cost of living for the rest of your life.**

  The biggest risk people face today and in the future is that their income will not rise at a pace that will keep them ahead of *taxes and inflation* for the *rest of their lives*.

- **Definition of Safety = Your income *will rise* for the rest of your life.**

  The safest investment investors can make is in the great companies in the U.S. and around the world. These companies' stocks will provide you with an excellent opportunity to make your principal and income rise for the rest of your life.

- **Stocks are safer than bonds.**

  Stocks are safer than bonds because, on average, they earn twice as much per year (11%). They are the only investment that has historically outpaced taxes and inflation.

- **Stocks can keep going up...**

  Stocks can keep going up forever (or at least for your lifetime) because all of us need the products companies make and sell.

- **No one can accurately predict the short-term direction of the market.**

  Why? Because most declines are triggered by completely unexpected events.

- **All financial advisors/brokers are not the same.**
  As in any profession, financial advisors have different education and experience levels. Look at both education and experience before hiring an advisor.

- **Traditional Diversification reduces fluctuation.**
  By diversifying with stocks, bonds, CDs and money market, investors can reduce overall portfolio fluctuation. The flip side? You also reduce return.

- **Accumulators of wealth love markets that are getting killed.**
  Investors who are accumulating wealth by adding money in regular intervals love fluctuation. The more often the fluctuation the better. The deeper the fluctuation the better. Would you rather buy tuna at $2.89 a can or $.75 a can?

- **Fluctuation is Not loss.**
  Fluctuation is not loss unless you make the *Big Mistake* and make a panicky sell decision. Fluctuation is only fluctuation – a temporary decline. *Ignore Chicken Little.*

- **There's no such thing as 'no risk'.**
  If your principal does not fluctuate (CDs), it is exposed to loss of purchasing power risk (this is a sure thing for the rest of your life). If your principal does fluctuate (by owning shares of America's great companies), it is exposed to temporary decline risk (this is temporary).

- **Your investment timeframe should be for the *rest of your life.***
  Excluding short-term goals, a significant portion of your money should be invested to support you for the rest of your life. You cannot afford to run out of money or income during your lifetime. *How long are you going to live?*

About the Author ... Dan Geffre

Dan Geffre has been a financial advisor with a national brokerage firm since 1989, becoming a firm partner in 1998. He is a licensed stockbroker, holding additional licenses in both life and health insurance and annuities.

Dan is completing a Master of Science Degree in Financial Services from the American College in Bryn Mawr, Pennsylvania. For the past eight years, he has been teaching community education classes in the fundamentals of investing.

Dan's business is located in Fargo, North Dakota, where he lives with his wife Jodi and son Grant.

If you are interested in Dan's educational seminars or classes, or if you have any comments about the book, please write to:

THE INVE$TOR FOR LIFE
PO BOX 9872
FARGO, ND 58106-9872